Sigrid Estrada

Ian Frazier is the author of nine books. A frequent contributor to *The New Yorker*, he lives in Montclair, New Jersey.

ALSO BY IAN FRAZIER

Dating Your Mom

Nobody Better, Better Than Nobody

Great Plains

Family

Coyote v. Acme

On the Rez

It Happened Like This (translator)

The Fish's Eye

Gone to New York

Lamentations
of the Father

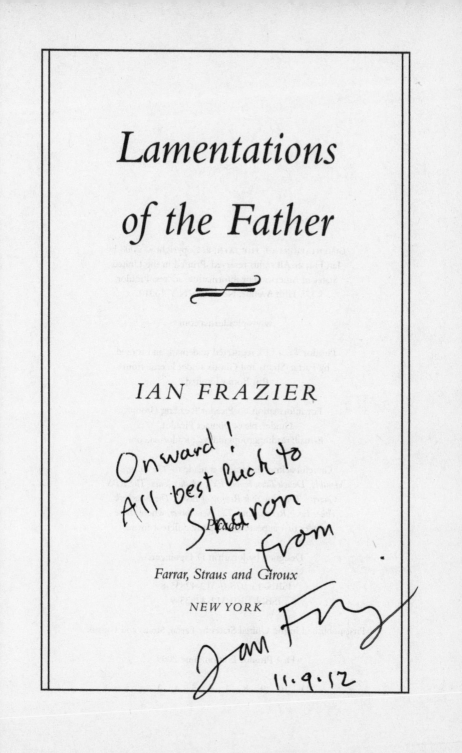

IAN FRAZIER

Onward !
All best luck to
Sharon
from

Farrar, Straus and Giroux

NEW YORK

Ian Fry

11.9.12

www.picadorusa.com

Picador® is a U.S. registered trademark and is used
by Farrar, Straus and Giroux under license from
Pan Books Limited.

For information on Picador Reading Group
Guides, please contact Picador.
E-mail: readinggroupguides@picadorusa.com

Grateful acknowledgment is made to *The Atlantic
Monthly, DoubleTake, Forbes FYI, Mother Jones, The RBS
Gazette, The New York Review of Books, The New York
Times Book Review,* and *The New Yorker,* where these
pieces first appeared, in slightly different form.

Designed by Jonathan D. Lippincott

ISBN-13: 978-0-312-42835-8
ISBN-10: 0-312-42835-9

First published in the United States by Farrar, Straus and Giroux

First Picador Edition: June 2009

D   10 9 8 7 6 5 4 3

To Bill and Tim McClelland

Contents

Lamentations
of the Father

Kisses All Around

Ad Martinum Lutherum
Doctorem Theologiae
Univ. Wittenberg
Saxonia, Germania

Sextus Februarius A.D. 1519

Fr. Martin, our brother beloved in Christ:

I bring you greetings for your good health from our blessed father, His Holiness Leo X.

His Holiness has instructed me to send you this letter of thanks for your very interesting "Ninety-five Theses," which you or perhaps a friend sent to us some months ago. He wishes to apologize for his slowness in replying to this work. He adds that it has a pleasing appearance, is well numbered, and shows the great skill of those who made it. Those new machines for printing that you Germans have built should help you to disseminate such writings widely.

Unfortunately, His Holiness has not yet been able to read through your theses with the care he would wish to give them. I can promise you that "Ninety-five Theses" is on the table next to his bed, and he will certainly get to it soon. As you know, this is a busy time on our ecclesiastical calendar, and he is required to attend several mystery plays every day. When he lies down in the evening and tries to read, in just a minute or two he has fallen asleep.

In truth, ninety-five theses are really a great many to expect him to read. Perhaps with some excision you could reduce your list to a mere four or five; then he could read them all with not so great an effort.

His Holiness also asks that I wish you good luck in the composition of other writings, in the grace of our Lord,

Michael Rintonius, O.S.A.

Amanuensis

•

Mr. John Peter Zenger, Esq.
New-York Weekly Journal
Broad Street, New-York City

Monday, September 23d, 1734

My Dear Sir,

As Governour of this fair Colony, I commend you for the Excellence of your Newspaper, justly famed among Citizens of our City for the Regularity of its Publication and the sprightly Contentiousness of its Views.

Tho I am told that it does truculently attack both Myself and Our Sovereign George II, I cannot say this to be true from Reading of it, as I receive all the News of Importance from the Town Crier and so make do without Newspaper at all.

However, please be assured that a big Pile of Journals awaits me still in my study, where I plan to sit down and read through them One by One, Occasion permitting, perhaps after Council adjourns next Spring.

Your most obliged, &c.

Col. William Cosby
Gov. Gen'l

•

M. Émile Zola
42, rue des Ormes
Paris, France

28 Juin 1898

Mon cher Émile,

J'adore "J'Accuse"! I congratulate you on the creation of this wonderful title you have devised for this new novella of yours. "J'Accuse"—what force, what audacity, what conciseness you have managed to convey in a single word printed so boldly there at the top of the page for all to see!

The quick perusal my schedule has so far permitted of your story seems to indicate that it has something to do with a young man in the army. Ahh—good! I have always enjoyed a fascinating war yarn! Although at the moment my wife is holding firmly to our only copy and refuses to give it up on pain of death, nevertheless, when she is finally finished, I anticipate reading it myself with the greatest pleasure.

Please accept the most sincere compliments from both Mme. Faure and myself. With that title alone you have joined the ranks of the immortals!

With greatest admiration,

Félix Faure
Président de la République

To: All Writers, Journalists, Editors, and
Publishers of the U.S.S.R.
From: The People's Commissariat for Internal
Affairs (N.K.V.D.)

12 August 193-

Comrades:

We officers and other workers of the N.K.V.D. join in unanimous praise to you for the remarkably large number of books, newspapers, magazines, privately circulated typewritten documents, and other works you have produced during the preceding year. We can tell that an absolutely enormous amount of labor must have gone into them. They look beautiful. Well done!

If you saw the enormous heaps of writings we have down here at the Lubyanka, you would understand why we cannot say for certain that we will be able to read everything in the near future, especially because we have only recently received a shipment of new Deanna Durbin films, which we must first screen. Unavoidably, it might take us quite a while to get back to you—at the rate we are going, perhaps even decades. We regret this extreme delay, and assure you that it does not reflect on the quality of your work, which is no doubt excellent.

From the desk of
A. R. KHOMEINI, Imam

11 Safar A.H. 1409

Salman—

Satanic looks great. They did a tremendous job on the cover, didn't they? You must be thrilled.

I can't wait to dive into it (it's as thick as four Korans!), and it's driving me crazy—here's what my week looks like: I've got the big party for the death of the Shah tomorrow night, then I spend two days racing around meeting the guys who flagellate themselves, then I have to judge a Jimmy Carter look-alike contest. And on and on.

If I don't have a chance to read your book right away, you'll forgive, yes? I give you my word I will do my absolute best to read it as soon as I can. Next vacation to Mecca, at the latest. Or else I'll bring it with me on the red-eye, next trip to Paris. Truly, I can sense already that this book is a creation of genius. In a strange way, I feel so in tune with it, it's as if I hardly have to read it for real.

Death to Bush or whoever,
and kisses all around,

Ruhi

Laws Concerning Food and Drink; Household Principles; Lamentations of the Father

O f the beasts of the field, and of the fishes of the sea, and of all foods that are acceptable in my sight you may eat, but not in the living room. Of the hoofed animals, broiled or ground into burgers, you may eat, but not in the living room. Of the cloven-hoofed animals, plain or with cheese, you may eat, but not in the living room. Of the cereal grains, of the corn and of the wheat and of the oats, and of all the cereals that are of bright color and unknown provenance you may eat, but not in the living room. Of the quiescently frozen dessert and of all frozen aftermeal treats you may eat, but absolutely not in the living room. Of the juices and other beverages, yes, even of those in sippy cups, you may drink, but not in the living room, neither may you carry such therein. Indeed, when you reach the place where the living room carpet begins, of any food or beverage there you may not eat, neither may you drink.

But if you are sick, and are lying down and watching something, then may you eat in the living room.

Laws When at Table

And if you are seated in your high chair, or in a chair such as a greater person might use, keep your legs and feet below you as they were. Neither raise up your knees, nor place your feet upon the table, for that is an abomination to me. Yes, even when you have an interesting bandage to show, your feet upon the table are an abomination, and worthy of rebuke. Drink your milk as it is given you, neither use on it any utensils, nor fork, nor knife, nor spoon, for that is not what they are for: if you will dip your blocks in the milk, and lick it off, you will be sent away. When you have drunk, let the empty cup then remain upon the table, and do not bite it upon its edge and by your teeth hold it to your face in order to make noises in it sounding like a duck; for you will be sent away.

When you chew your food, keep your mouth closed until you have swallowed, and do not open it to show your brother or your sister what is within; I say to you, do not so, even if your brother or your sister has done the same to you. Eat your food only; do not eat that which is not food; neither seize the table between your jaws, nor use the raiment of the table to wipe your lips. I say again to you, do not touch it, but leave it as it is. And though your stick of carrot does indeed resemble a marker, draw not with it upon the table, even in pretend, for we do not do that, that is why. And though the pieces of broccoli are very like small trees, do not stand them upright to make a forest, because we do not do that, that is why. Sit just as I have told you, and do not lean to one side or the other, nor slide down until you are nearly slid away. Heed me; for if you sit like that, your hair will go into the syrup. And now behold, even as I have said, it has come to pass.

Laws Pertaining to Dessert

For we judge between the plate that is unclean and the plate that is clean, saying first, if the plate is clean, then you shall have dessert. But of the unclean plate, the laws are these: If you have eaten most of your meat, and two bites of your peas, with each bite consisting of not fewer than three peas each, or in total six peas, eaten where I can see, and you have also eaten enough of your potatoes to fill two forks, both forkfuls eaten where I can see, then you shall have dessert. But if you eat a lesser number of peas, and yet you eat the potatoes, still you shall not have dessert; and if you eat the peas, yet leave the potatoes uneaten, you shall not have dessert, no, not even a small portion thereof. And if you try to deceive by moving the potatoes or peas around with a fork, that it may appear you have eaten what you have not, you will fall into iniquity. And I will know, and you shall have no dessert.

On Screaming

Do not scream; for it is as if you scream all the time. If you are given a plate on which two foods you do not wish to touch each other are touching each other, your voice rises up even to the ceiling, while you point to the offense with the finger of your right hand; but I say to you, scream not, only remonstrate gently with the server, that the server may correct the fault. Likewise if you receive a portion of fish from which every piece of herbal seasoning has not been scraped off, and the herbal seasoning is loathsome to you, and steeped in vileness, again I say, refrain from screaming. Though the vileness overwhelm you, and cause you a faint unto death, make not that sound from within your throat, neither cover your face, nor press your fingers to your nose. For even now I have made the fish as it should be; behold, I eat of it myself, yet do not die.

Concerning Face and Hands

Cast your countenance upward to the light, and lift your eyes to the hills, that I may more easily wash you off. For the stains are upon you; even to the very back of your head, there is rice thereon. And in the breast pocket of your garment, and upon the tie of your shoe, rice and other fragments are distributed in a manner wonderful to see. Only hold yourself still; hold still, I say. Give each finger in its turn for my examination thereof, and also each thumb. Lo, how iniquitous they appear. What I do is as it must be; and you shall not go hence until I have done.

Various Other Laws, Statutes, and Ordinances

Bite not, lest you be cast into quiet time. Neither drink of your own bathwater, nor of bathwater of any kind; nor rub your feet on bread, even if it be in the package; nor rub yourself against cars, nor against any building; nor eat sand.

Leave the cat alone, for what has the cat done, that you should so afflict it with tape? And hum not that humming in your nose as I read, nor stand between the light and the book. Indeed, you will drive me to madness. Nor forget what I said about the tape.

Complaints and Lamentations

O my children, you are disobedient. For when I tell you what you must do, you argue and dispute hotly even to the littlest detail; and when I do not accede, you cry out, and hit and kick. Yes, and even sometimes do you spit, and shout "stupid-head" and other blasphemies, and hit and kick the wall and the molding thereof when you are sent to the corner. And though the law teaches that no one shall be sent to the corner for more minutes than he has years of age, yet I would leave you there all day, so mighty am I in anger. But upon being sent to the corner you ask straightaway, "Can I come out?" and I reply, "No, you may not come out." And again you ask, and again I give the same reply. But when you ask again a third time, then you may come out.

Hear me, O my children, for the bills they kill me. I pay and pay again, even to the twelfth time in a year, and yet again they mount higher than before. For our health, that we may be covered, I give six hundred and twenty talents twelve times in a year; but even this covers not the fifteen hundred deductible for each member of the family within a calendar year. And yet for ordinary visits we still are not covered, nor for many medicines, nor for the teeth within our mouths. Guess not at what rage is in my mind, for surely you cannot know.

For I will come to you at the first of the month and at the fifteenth of the month with the bills and a great whining and moan. And when the month of taxes comes, I will decry the wrong and unfairness of it, and mourn with wine and ashtrays, and rend my receipts. And you shall remember that I am that I am: before, after, and until you are twenty-one. Hear me then, and avoid me in my wrath, O children of me.

Tomorrow's Bird

S ince May, I've been working for the crows, and so far
it's the best job I've ever had. I kind of fell into it by a
combination of preparedness and luck. I'd been casting
around a bit, looking for a new direction in my career, and one
afternoon when I was out on my walk, I happened to see some
crows fly by. One of them landed on a telephone wire just
above my head. I looked at him for a moment, and then on
impulse I made a *skchhh* noise with my teeth and lips. He
seemed to like that; I saw his tail make a quick upward bobbing
motion at the sound. Encouraged, I made the noise again, and
again his tail bobbed. He looked at me closely with one eye,
then turned his beak and looked at me with the other, meanwhile readjusting his feet on the wire. After a few minutes, he
cawed and flew off to join his companions. I had a good feeling I couldn't put into words. Basically, I thought the meeting
had gone well, and as it turned out, I was right. When I got
home there was a message from the crows saying I had the job.

That first interview proved indicative of the crows' business
style. They are very informal and relaxed, unlike their public
persona, and mostly they leave me alone. I'm given a general
direction of what they want done, but the specifics of how to

do it are up to me. For example, the crows have long been unhappy about public misperceptions of them: that they raid other birds' nests, drive songbirds away, eat garbage and dead things, can't sing, etc., all of which are completely untrue once you know them. My first task was to take these misperceptions and turn them into a more positive image. I decided the crows needed a slogan that emphasized their strengths as a species. The slogan I came up with was "Crows: We Want to Be Your Only Bird™." I told this to the crows, they loved it, and we've been using it ever since.

Crows speak a dialect of English rather like that of the remote hill people of the Alleghenies. If you're not accustomed to it, it can be hard to understand. In their formal speech they are as measured and clear as a radio announcer from the Midwest—though, as I say, they are seldom formal with me. (For everyday needs, of course, they caw.) Their unit of money is the empty soda bottle, which trades at a rate of about twenty to the dollar. In the recent years of economic boom, the crows have quietly amassed great power. With investment capital based on their nationwide control of everything that gets run over on the roads, they have bought a number of major companies. Pepsi-Cola is now owned by the crows, as well as Knight Ridder Newspapers and the company that makes Tombstone frozen pizzas. New York's Metropolitan Opera is now wholly crow-owned.

In order to stay competitive, as most people know, the crows recently merged with the ravens. This was done not only for reasons of growth but also to better serve those millions who live and work near crows. In the future, both crows and ravens will be known by the group name of Crows, so if you see a bird and wonder which it is, you don't have to waste any time: officially and legally, it's a crow. The net result of this, of course, is that now there are a lot more crows—which is exactly what the crows want. Studies they've sponsored show that there could be anywhere from ten to a thousand times more crows than there already are, with no strain on carrying capacity. A healthy increase in crow numbers would make basic services like cawing loudly outside your bedroom window at six in the morning available to all. In this area, as in many others, the crows are thinking very long-term.

If more people in the future get a chance to know crows as I have done, they are in for a real treat. Because, I must say, the crows have been absolutely wonderful to me. I like them not just as highly profitable business associates but as friends. Their aggressive side, admittedly quite strong in disputes with scarlet tanagers, etc., has been nowhere in evidence around me. I could not wish for any companions more charming. The other day I was having lunch with an important crow in the park, me sipping from a drinking fountain while he ate peanuts taken from a squirrel. In between sharp downward raps of his bill on the peanut shell to poke it open, he drew me out with seemingly artless questions. Sometimes the wind would push the shell to one side and he would steady it with one large foot while continuing the raps with his beak. And all the while, he kept up his attentive questioning, making me feel that, business considerations aside, he was truly interested in what I had to say.

"Crows: We Want to Be Your Only Bird™." I think this slogan is worth repeating, because there's a lot behind it. Of course, the crows don't literally want (or expect) to be the only species of bird left on the planet. They admire and enjoy other kinds of birds and even hope that there will still be some remaining in limited numbers out of doors as well as in zoos and museums. But in terms of daily usage, the crows hope that you will think of them first when you're looking for those quality-of-life intangibles usually associated with birds. Singing, for example: crows actually can sing, and beautifully, too; however, so far they have not been given any chance. In the future, with fewer other birds around, they feel that they will be.

Whether they're good-naturedly harassing an owl caught out in daylight, or carrying bits of sticks and used gauze bandage in their beaks to make their colorful, free-form nests, or simply landing on the sidewalk in front of you with their characteristic double hop, the crows have become a part of the fabric of our days. When you had your first kiss, the crows were there, flying around nearby. They were cawing overhead at your college graduation, and worrying a hamburger wrapper through the wire mesh of a trash container in front of the building when you went in for your first job interview, and flapping past the door of the hospital where you held your firstborn child. The crows have always been with us, and they promise that by growing the species at a predicted rate of 17 percent a year, in the future they'll be around even more.

The crows aren't the last Siberian tigers, and they don't pretend to be. They're not interested in being a part of anybody's dying tradition. But then, how many of us deal with Siberian tigers on a regular basis? Usually, the nontech stuff we deal with, besides humans, is squirrels, pigeons, raccoons, rats, mice, and a few kinds of bugs. The crows are confident enough to claim that they will be able to compete effectively even with these familiar and well-entrenched providers. Indeed, they have already begun to displace pigeons in the category of walking around under park benches with chewing gum stuck to their feet. Scampering nervously in attics, sneaking through pet doors, and gnawing little holes in things are all in the crows' expansion plans.

I would not have taken this job if I did not believe, strongly and deeply, in the crows myself. And I do. I could go on and on about the crows' generosity, taste in music, sense of family values, the "buddy system" they invented to use against other birds, the work they do for the Shriners, and more. But they're paying me a lot of bottles to say this—I can't expect everybody to believe me. I do ask, if you're unconvinced, that you take this simple test: Next time you're looking out a window or driving in a car, notice if there's a crow in sight. Then multiply that one crow by lots and lots of crows, and you'll get an idea of what the next years will bring. In the bird department, no matter what, the future is going to be almost all crows, almost all the time. That's just a fact.

So why not just accept it, and learn to appreciate it, as so many of us have already? The crows are going to influence our culture and our world in beneficial ways we can't even imagine today. Much of what they envision I am not yet at liberty to disclose, but I can tell you that it is magnificent. They are going to be birds like we've never seen. In their dark, jewel-like eyes burns an ambition to be more and better and to fly around all over the place constantly. They're smart, they're driven, and they're comin' at us. The crows: let's get ready to welcome tomorrow's only bird.

Little House off the Highway

The prairie grasses rippled in the warm spring wind as Laura ran down the trail past the lookout post above her family's cabin on the banks of the Big Ravine. Puffs of dust rose under her bare feet as she hurried. The sound of wheels in the gravel of the long drive told her that company was coming, and Laura wanted to see who it could be. Laura was a big girl now, almost nine. Pa called her "little half-pint" and said she wasn't any bigger than an IRS agent's heart. But she was wiry, and strong for a girl.

Laura loved living here out away from town, and she loved the family's new cabin. Pa had bartered some surplus equipment for it, and he and his friend Mr. Ettinger had moved it here on two hay wagons when the roads firmed up in late fall. Ma had been glad to get out of the school bus into a real house for a change. She had polished the floors and painted the walls until they gleamed. The new cabin had plenty of room for everybody: Pa, Ma, Laura, her three sisters, and Jack, the family's brindle-faced bulldog. Jack looked very fierce, but never bit unless you had a tie or a uniform on.

Just last week a man who worked for the so-called state of North Dakota had come to the cabin with a paper that he said authorized him to take Jack away. Luckily, some friends were visiting Pa that day, and together they had faced the man down and made him leave empty-handed. Laura hoped that the dust she saw coming up the drive wasn't him returning. Pa had said he wouldn't be so polite the next time. Jack ran out from under the porch, barking and growling as usual, and then suddenly he stopped barking and his tail began to wag. At the same moment Laura recognized the bright blue eyes, bushy beard, and cheerful grin of Red Bandanna Doe, an old friend of the family's whose real name only Pa knew for sure. Mr. Doe climbed down from the driver's seat, slapped the dust from his trousers with his jungle hat, and grabbed Jack and Laura in a big bear hug.

"Why, Mr. Doe, I declare!" said Ma, opening the cabin door and wiping her hands on her fatigues. "We didn't expect to see you again until the new moon!"

"Well, ma'am," he replied with a quiet smile, "you know I never follow any set routine, for reasons of my own."

"Yes, I suppose that's so," Ma said, and for an instant a thoughtful look filled her soft blue eyes. "Charles is shredding papers out back," she continued. "Pull up a chair here on the porch in the sun, and I'll tell him you're here."

Mr. Doe had seceded from "the United States" last New Year's, but to Laura he still seemed just the same. He still smelled like cinnamon and tobacco and gun solvent, and he still carried the sweets in his many pockets which Laura and the little girls liked to clamber on him to find. Laura stood apart shyly as Carrie and Baby Grace, giggling, searched for the candies. She was too old for that now.

Just then Pa came striding around the corner of the cabin, a merry grin lighting up his sparkling blue eyes. "Why, Doe, I'll be derned!" Pa said, taking him by the hand.

"Charles, please, don't swear," Ma reminded, following a step behind.

Pa apologized. Then he and Mr. Doe embraced and slapped each other on the back and laughed, and Mr. Doe called Pa "Number 17," an old custom between them that Laura didn't completely understand. After a few minutes they went inside the cabin to talk privately, while Ma and Laura and her sisters stayed outside on the porch.

Pa and Mr. Doe had met at an estate auction last summer and liked each other right away. Pa said Mr. Doe had the best head for figures of any man he ever knew. Since spring ice-out Pa and Mr. Doe had been hatching some complicated, secret scheme, Laura was sure. But whenever she asked Pa about it, he just laughed a big laugh that split his black beard and showed his white teeth. Pa had a laugh that boomed and roared and echoed; and it made Laura feel warm all over. When she heard it, she knew that nothing could be wrong in the world.

"We're living in the last days, Doe." Pa's voice rose from downstairs with the smell of the morning coffee as Laura snuggled under the quilts in her bedroom below the eaves. Sleepily she wondered if Pa and his friend had gotten up early, or had never gone to bed the night before. "All the signs are there," she heard Pa continue. "Portents in the heavens, universal daylight savings, the frug . . ." It was lovely drifting in and out of sleep to the gentle sound of grown-ups' voices, knowing that she didn't have to go to school.

What did Laura need with school, anyway? She liked having lots of free time, and going to gun shows with Pa, and reading the many interesting pamphlets he received in the mail. Now he was talking about the sheep being divided from the goats and the graves opening up and releasing their dead. Pa always had a way of putting things that made you see exactly what he meant.

Suddenly Laura's china-blue eyes popped wide open as she remembered what day this was. She had almost forgotten! Pa had promised that today she could help him and Mr. Doe mix fuel oil with little pellets of fertilizer in fifty-five-gallon drums for a project they were working on. Pa had said it was an important job that required great care. You had to see that the oil coated each pellet just so, not too much and not too little. He wouldn't trust the job to any of her sisters or even to Ma, he said. Laura glowed with pleasure to think that he had chosen her. In a single bound she leaped from bed, wiggled into her clothes, and clambered down the ladder to her place at the breakfast table.

"Well, you're up early, Laura," Pa greeted her, grinning a grin even bigger than his usual one. Jack, lying on the floor by Pa's chair, barked cheerfully, and his nearly blue eyes sparkled with excitement, because he knew he was to be taken along on the day's adventure, too. When all had eaten their fill of Ma's clabber cakes, buttermilk, and dietary supplements, Laura and Pa and Mr. Doe and Jack got into a loaner wagon Pa had obtained from his company. Then they went down the dusty driveway and along the road to a seldom-used rest area on Highway 9.

So one day followed another in this wild new land, where people like Pa could settle down at last and be free. Laura and her sisters soon made many friends among their distant neighbors after they had been cleared by Pa. They went on picnics and held socials, prayer meetings, and sing-alongs. Sometimes Pa had to take trips to Nevada to look for extra work in the hotels there. Those weeks were hard for the family, all alone in the cabin without his friendly words telling them what to do. But then suddenly he would return, filling the whole doorway in his big buffalo coat, handing out treats for the little ones and brightly colored magazines and lottery tickets for Ma.

People who had lived for years by the Big Ravine said that the winters there had gotten shorter, the springs and summers longer, and the storms more severe. Laura was too young to judge whether or not that was true. She knew, however, that the flocks of Canada geese appeared in the sky overhead every fall, passing in long skeins like giant check marks upon the clouds only to land nearby and not go anywhere, and that the dun-colored mule deer were plentiful in the draws and on the roads, and that a multitude of crows and ravens and starlings beyond numbering gathered on the burnished land year in and year out no matter what the weather was.

Laura did not care what people said. She may have been only eight years old, but somehow she understood that everyone should just do for himself. Her heart filled with joy as she stood on the bluff above the interstate and looked out across the prairie while the rising wind pressed her dress and petticoats against her knees. She breathed deep of the crisp, dusty air and almost shouted with a sudden surge of pride. This was where she belonged, even if the cities were better and had plumbing and so on. She had become a part of this place, and it of her, and here she would remain until she was grown or could get a part-time job in Bismarck or maybe Minneapolis–St. Paul.

Th-Th-That's Not All, Folks

> *Gladiator* [the movie] is a big hit, but is it historically accurate? . . . How much of *Gladiator* is actually true?
> —*Newsweek*, May 14, 2000

Yes, there was an actual duck on which the well-known screen character was based. He did not have a name; around the poultry shed where he nested, he had only a number, like all the other black ducks, but today there are conflicting stories about what the number was. His original owner says it was 27, but that could be wrong. Everyone who knew him agrees that nobody on the farm ever called him Daffy, and that some scriptwriter must have thought that up. The pig was based on a real pig named Porky Pig who lived on the farm and died in 1989. He wore the little narrow-brimmed hat and bow tie only on special occasions, and the rest of the time he just rooted around in the mud with the other pigs. The fact that the fictional version of him became famous did not affect him at all. The stutter was a complete fabrication added by Hollywood to make him more interesting. The real pig did not stutter and spoke rarely or never, depending on who you ask.

Elmer Fudd, a patent attorney and amateur sportsman from Covina, California, was the inspiration for the character of that name. Fudd served four terms as state senator, so much of his life is a matter of public record, easy to check. When you dig a little deeper into some of the stories about him, however, you find that a lot of fudging of the facts has been going on. For example, in his passion for hunting he did shoot at several of the animals, including the duck, on a number of occasions. But according to a veterinarian's report filed June 8, 1959, a blast fired by Fudd point-blank at the duck's face left No. 27 (or Daffy) with birdshot pellets embedded in the front of the skull, as well as a partially perforated eardrum on the left side. In the film version of this incident, the full force of the gun blast strikes the duck squarely on the bill, causing the bill to spin quickly around the duck's head for perhaps two dozen rotations and come to rest at the back of the duck's head rather than the front. According to the best information we have found so far, this did not occur.

Other accounts of the doings of Fudd and his cronies play similarly fast and loose with the truth. A case in point is the portrait of Fudd's cinematic colleague Yosemite Sam (sic—no last name given). This character appears to have been closely modeled on a man named Robert "Yellowstone Bob" Skinner, a rancher and sometime stuntman in the Sacramento area forty-odd years ago, whom many local residents remember well. Like his cinematic counterpart, Skinner was short, had a long red mustache that drooped almost to his feet, wore big boots and an oversize brown cowboy hat, and carried two six-shooters. Also like the screen version, Skinner used to hop up and down when angry and fire both his pistols simultaneously into the ground on either side of him, kicking up lots of dust, while megaphone-shaped bursts of steam shot out of both his ears. All of those details we have been able to verify from people who were there. Many other aspects of his behavior as depicted on film, however, are apparently unsubstantiated. On-screen, for example, when this character becomes annoyed at something one of the other characters has done, he often exclaims, "Ton-sarn that varmint!" Unfortunately, no one who knew Skinner remembers him ever saying such a thing. Several recalled that occasionally he used to say, "Oh, Christ, Audrey—now what?" (Audrey was Skinner's second wife.) Such inconsistencies the makers of the film apparently felt free to disregard.

Most troubling, from the point of view of real-life accuracy, is the character of the rabbit. His inappropriate name (Bugs? Why that, for a rabbit?) is just one of many questions still unresolved. To make matters more confusing, on-screen he sometimes dresses as the duck or as a beautiful woman to fool the hunter (Fudd), while at other times he appears as a bull-fighter, a newspaper reporter, a Viking maiden, or the conductor of a symphony orchestra. The viewer is left wondering: Who, exactly, is he?

Our findings show that the character of the rabbit was actually a composite portrait based on several backyard rabbits who lived in greater Los Angeles during the late 1930s and early 1940s. One of these rabbits had very long ears, another had large white feet, another had two big front upper incisors, another was constantly chewing on carrots, and so on. Trying to pin down which real rabbit is the source for which on-screen exploit, however, is no easy task. Here one enters a hall of mirrors where truths, half-truths, and total falsehoods mix and mingle in a kaleidoscopic whirl as reality slips maddeningly out of reach. Most of the rabbits' neighbors and other witnesses who could be of help have moved away or died. The memories of those few who remain are quite vague, perhaps unavoidably so, perhaps for some other reason. If, as the movie version claims, the rabbit and the duck once accidentally burrowed (!) into a cave full of treasure belonging to a sultan and got into a fight with a muscular guard named Hassan, and then a genie shrunk the duck down to a tiny size, and the duck went running off into the distance holding a diamond bigger than himself and screaming in a tiny voice how rich he was, this alleged event left no tangible physical evidence that we could find. If one of the original rabbits on which the cinematic rabbit was supposedly based did, in fact, dress in a tuxedo and pass himself off as Leopold Stokowski and conduct a symphony orchestra and make one of the singers hold a note so long that the singer's face turned several colors, and the proscenium arch directly overhead began to crumble, and the cracks in the proscenium spread, and pieces began to fall down, and the whole auditorium eventually collapsed—where, then, is the documentation? Are there program notes of the concert, newspaper stories about the disaster at the concert hall, insurance appraisals of the damage, and so on?

Confronted with these questions, the studio has so far stonewalled. To date, its only response has been a terse two-line statement saying that although hard proof of certain events may not be immediately available, at least they "could have" occurred. Sadly, "could have" is not good enough for those of us demanding factual accountability. Granted, the rabbit "could

have" gone into outer space and prevented a small Martian
with a strange accent from blowing up the earth—the earth is
still here, after all. Careful observers, however, will withhold
judgment until more evidence comes to light. Meanwhile, the
misquotations, distortions, and deliberate misrepresentations of
the facts as purveyed on-screen have already done a serious dis-
service to the people and animals from whose lives these facts
were drawn. In fairness to everybody, reality can only be what
really occurred, and nothing more. As responsible viewers and
citizens, we must keep on the alert to make sure that the supposed "reality" offered by films and the media is, in fact, actually true.

My Wife Liz

In the mid-1970s, I was married for a time to the actress Elizabeth Taylor. If this information comes as news to you, join the crowd. Our marriage, though admittedly brief, was quite legal and official; today, however, it remains virtually unknown to the public at large. Ask anyone about Ms. Taylor's husbands and you'll get the usual recitation of Mike Todd and Eddie Fisher and Richard Burton and John Warner and so on, with never a mention of me. Now, I don't care if I'm famous or not, and I have no financial ax to grind. All the same, it hurts to be left out. The feelings Ms. Taylor and I had for each other did not last, it's true; but while we were together, we were a part of show-business history every bit as real as any other marriage she had. I have only affection and good memories when I think of Ms. Taylor today. But when I think of how I have been overlooked as one of her husbands, I feel anger, indignation, and a strong desire to see justice done.

Some people say that there should be certain minimum standards you have to meet in order to qualify as an ex-husband of Elizabeth Taylor's, and that I (and a few other guys) don't make the grade. Utter garbage! A person would have to be pitifully naive not to see the fine hand of the distinguished

Senator Warner in this power grab. He even tried to ram a law through Congress to that effect, with a lot of legalistic fine print about the length of the marriage in calendar days, number of tabloid articles about the marriage, and so on (all of which favors his own claims, by the way). I regret to say that in California a similar law actually passed the legislature and went into effect in 1999. By its criteria, Larry Fortensky, a husband from the 1990s, qualifies and I don't. I like Larry, and I respect him as a fellow ex. But all I can say is, look at the facts and do the math: if *he* was married to Elizabeth Taylor, *I* was married to Elizabeth Taylor.

Now, for the record, here is how it was between Liz and me. The year was 1974. I had just got out of college and was living with my parents, and trying to rekindle a relationship with Jayna Mills, my girlfriend from high school. One night I was dialing her number when accidentally I instead called Elizabeth Taylor. With my mind on something else, I happened to dial a number in Beverly Hills which turned out to be hers. I recognized her voice immediately. In those days she had just divorced Richard Burton and was dating the scientist and peace activist Linus Pauling, but he was pretty old, and she had a lot of time on her hands. Why she didn't hang up on me—I was, after all, a wrong number—I'll never know, but somehow we fell into conversation that became warm and familiar after only a few minutes. Not many people know what a wonderful listener Liz can be. Before I realized it, I was telling her everything about Jayna's and my romance, and how she had dumped me for one of the Four Speeds (a local band) while I was off at school. For her part, Liz went into some of the problems she was having with Dr. Pauling, who may have won the Nobel

Peace Prize but who was also a complicated person in many ways. I guess neither Liz nor I had really known before how lonely we were. Before we hung up, we exchanged phone numbers and agreed to talk again soon.

Well, that was the beginning. The very next evening I called her again, and our conversation was even better than the first one. I began calling her almost every single night in a long-distance telephone courtship that continued for months. Liz and I told each other secrets we had never told anybody. Working for Davey Tree Company and living in Ohio, I was, for Liz, a safe listener in whom she could confide her true feelings about the Hollywood world. And for me Liz was—I really can't describe the happiness that Liz was for me.

When the phone bills began to come in, and my parents had a look at them, they were very concerned. I offered to pay the bills myself, even though they took up my whole salary and more. And I tried, the best I could, to explain to my parents about Elizabeth Taylor and me. They were overwhelmed, naturally. They just could not get used to the fact that their son was romancing this famous person every night on their downstairs phone. It was a shaky time for us all. Plus, right around then we started getting a lot of strange calls—hangups, breathing, funny noises—which I cannot prove came from Linus Pauling, though I believe to this day that they did. Finally, my mom and dad, God bless them, decided that if this was what I wanted, then okay. A customer of Dad's had a condo in Venice, California, and my parents arranged for me to house-sit there for a while and see what happened with this Liz business, since clearly it wasn't going to go away.

Events moved swiftly after my arrival. Liz and I decided we

had to be together all the time, and got engaged. The wedding was small—just me, Liz, my folks, Roddy McDowall, and Liz's longtime friend and publicist, Chen Sam. It took place before a judge in the Orange County Courthouse on December 10, 1974, at two in the afternoon. I find it worse than frustrating that now, through some bureaucratic mix-up, the county seems to have lost all record of the marriage. As for my own copy of the marriage certificate, it unfortunately disappeared with many of my other possessions in the sinking of my houseboat during the great Mississippi River floods of 1993.

Item: a photo of Liz and me coming down the courthouse steps; she is wearing a peach-colored suit and a little pink hat, and I am looking off to the side so you can't quite see my face. Item: a note to me, undated—"Dear, The automatic-opener thing on the garage door is stuck or something. Can you get someone to fix? Love always, L." Item: the stubs of a pair of tickets to a rock festival I took Liz to in the early days of our marriage; it was I, in fact, who introduced her to this exciting new music form. How little history leaves us, in the end! The only hard evidence of my marriage to Liz is these random keepsakes I happened to come across recently in the glove compartment of my van. They may not amount to much, but they're precious to me.

My lawyers have them now. I'm told that the more proof I can produce, the better. I regret that lawyers had to become involved, but I don't see that there was any choice. I needed someone to make my case for me; I'm too close to it to do it effectively all alone. Plus, it looks as if we're going to have to pursue this thing on a state-by-state basis, which could be a drawn-out process. On my own I've worked to get more publicity for my cause. I've gone on several radio call-in shows, trying to establish myself in the public's mind as an ex-husband of Elizabeth Taylor's. So far I don't know whether it's working. I thought I saw a sign of progress the other day when I noticed a woman I took to be a fan outside my house, apparently stalking me. When I confronted her, however, it turned out she had me confused with somebody else. I didn't get discouraged; I knew when I began the fight that I might be in for a long haul.

You don't go through an experience like mine without learning an important truth or two. Most important, I've come to like who I am. Who I am is a person who evidently was married briefly to Elizabeth Taylor but almost no one will admit it, so he has to get across to a bunch of self-important John Warner types a simple fact that shouldn't be such a big deal making me talk myself hoarse like this. I've also learned that that's not such a bad person to be. In general, I am at peace with myself, except when I get mad and carried away. Other than that, I'm always the same. You see, having once been married to Elizabeth Taylor gave me a great gift that no one can take from me: a calm knowledge of something too high and ideal even to have a name. When I can get a majority of the country to begin to accept what I'm saying, I'll be fine.

Walking Tour

The city has always been here, its proud inhabitants will tell you. Since before the last great ice sheets departed the European continent, human beings have dwelled on this gentle eminence above the mouth of the Imber River, where the "salubrious exhalations" (Stendhal) of the Pripet Marshes mingle with the cooling winds sweeping from the Alps and the Pyrenees. Some indefinable quality of the surrounding sky, a peculiar vividness of its light, seems to call forth civilization. Primitive tribes stopped here to graze their flocks and build their huts of stone and mammoth ivory; later the legions of Julius Caesar, extending Rome's imperium, fortified the site with walls, towers, and an ingenious aqueduct, parts of which still stand. Century upon century of human endeavor, the soaring cathedrals of the Middle Ages giving way to modern American-style high-rises, created the splendid city spread out before you today.

It's a city one peels back, layer after layer. According to many admirers, not even a lifetime is long enough to experience it all. Naturally, how much of the city a visitor sees depends on how much time he or she can spend. If you choose, you can explore the city by trolleybus, metro, hired car, or (in certain months) guided helicopter tour. Your schedule will of course determine your mode of transportation. For our money, however, the best way to see the city is as its most infatuated visitors always have—slowly, savoringly, with an itinerary of leisurely meandering, and, most important, on foot. The routes suggested below may be used by all kinds of travelers; we admit without apology that they favor the pedestrian.

City Center and Castle Enclave

Begin your tour where the city itself began, in the cobbled square (Fontanka Ploschad) surrounding the fountain of Neptune, original site of the artesian well that supplied the defenders during the siege of the city by Alaric and his Visigoths in A.D. 401. The multi-figured composition of dolphins, sea nymphs, hippocampi, and Tritons is a signature of the famous fountain designer Bartolomeo Torrelli, whose mother was the mistress of Charlemagne. Keeping the fountain on your left, proceed to the eastern entry of the castle at the gate to the outer rampart (admission 250 groschen, credit and debit cards accepted). This is the former periphery of the ancient city, whose massive stone structures served in later years as a prison and a meeting place of the first Constituent Assembly. Parts of the castle were heavily damaged during World War II and are permanently closed.

A museum in the former throne chamber houses a collection of church and state treasures, including diadems, scepters, reliquaries, and flails. The miter worn by Saint Vitus at his ordination is in a case at the center of the hall. Beyond the museum is a grassy courtyard cluttered with statuary of many periods, and farther still is a walkway always bustling with tourists and local people coming and going from the many points of departure at the city's core. Here self-employed craftsmen, buskers, and berry sellers compete for the busy trade. Here also you may encounter a cheerful young woman in a bright green T-shirt and baseball cap passing out free boxes of Tic Tac candies, small oval mint-flavored capsules made in North America. Competing for the candy market dominated by Life Savers, a venerable American brand, Tic Tac has frequently promoted itself during the past thirty years with vigorous advertising campaigns involving similar free-sample giveaways.

The Cathedral of Saint Martha-Sophia, looming above the metro station opposite, honors the city's patron and protector, believed to have saved some of the population during the plagues of 1576, 1598, and 1611. The cathedral's fire-gilded dome was carted off in sections by invading Swedes under Charles XII, but was later returned. An allegorical mosaic of the saint rescuing a sinner from a runaway horse representing lust enlivens the ceiling of the narthex. Elaborate inner doors of Renaissance gold filigree lead to the cathedral's cavernous nave, once the largest in the world, whose roof of high groined arches is supported by sixty-four columns of native marble. Imagine, if you will, the thousands of patient workmen who sawed these columns from living rock using the crude tools of that time. Small pieces of this same marble, ideal for paperweights and memo holders, may be purchased at the gift shop by the cathedral's side door.

The gift shop, in its nondescript kiosk of obviously recent construction, also sells postcards of the cathedral, small fringed flags bearing the city's coat of arms, commemorative snow globes, and other items. To divert the shop's young attendant, a radio in the kiosk is constantly playing popular music such as "The Shoop Shoop Song (It's in His Kiss)," by Cher. Cher, a late-twentieth-century American singer and actress, had her first popular hit with her singing partner and then-husband, Sonny Bono, in 1965. Their plangent ballad of young love, "I Got You Babe," gained them wide recognition and, briefly, a network television show of their own. After the TV show they divorced. Cher married one or two other rock stars, while Sonny Bono ran for and was elected to the U.S. House of Representatives as a Republican from the state of California, only to die in a skiing accident some years later. Cher is best known for her long, straight black hair, her penchant for baring her midriff, and the alluring charm of her navel. "The Shoop Shoop Song (It's in His Kiss)" dates from later in her career, c. 1991. (It was, of course, a remake of a much earlier hit by the R & B singer Betty Everett.) As you listen, turn again to the cathedral dome, which, thanks to an inspired placement of slate-gray shingles on the pitched roof just below it, often seems to float fantastically unmoored in the pewter-colored sky.

Business District and Market Row

Hard by the city's center is a busy commercial neighborhood extending for a mile or more along William Tell Prospekt. In the eighteenth century this area was called Englishtown (Anglischeburg), after the many merchants of that nationality who came here to buy furs and hemp. The disastrous Revised Economic Directive of the 1930s bulldozed every third building and replaced them all with blocks of solid cement, which have proved troublesome to remove. Though visitors in the recent past have complained of a lack of quality merchandise and a poor selection of colors and styles, you'll find the shopping situation better now.

Wear comfortable shoes, take your time, and don't be afraid to bargain. At the motley open-air stalls (*isby*) that line the curb, prices are so low that you'll have a hard time keeping a straight face as you do. That's part of the fun. Farther on, crowds thin out as you enter an area of expensive shops that have taken over what once were grand city houses for the aristocracy. A riot of Neo-Baroque terra-cotta bas-reliefs depicting scenes from the hunt adorn the front of No. 128, where the fabulously wealthy Von Hoffman family used to hold their glittering parties; now it houses an Italian clothing concern. Note the twin Atlases, beautifully restored, that support on their broad shoulders the frieze of acanthus leaves over the door to the cell phone outlet across the street at No. 131. When this building was a gentleman's club, it served as a frequent trysting place for Albert Einstein's barber and the legendary actress Sarah Bernhardt.

A Word About Crime

In general, the city is now very safe, despite what you have heard. Yes, the occasional band of Gypsies does sweep down upon unwary visitors, swarming with chattering tongues and quick hands, but they are easily deterred by buttoning up your pockets and standing very stiffly until they eventually go away. In the upscale shopping districts where you are likely to be, city officials are careful to provide plenty of police officers. In addition, most of the better food stores (*magaziny*) hire their own armed security staffs. In the fancy groceries, for example, young, blond ex-soldiers with up-to-date automatic weapons stand guard over racks selling imported breakfast foods like Müeslix, cinnamon-and-apple-flavored Quaker Instant Oatmeal, Cap'n Crunch, and Froot Loops, whose sky-high price tags put them beyond the reach of everybody except wealthy visitors and local criminal gangs.

Froot Loops, in particular, have a long association with crime. Introduced in the early 1960s, when Kellogg's, the American breakfast-food giant, was trying to move away from its rather staid products like Corn Flakes and All-Bran and into cereals with high sugar content deliberately aimed at children, Froot Loops immediately won a large market share, thanks mainly to a saturation campaign of television advertising featuring a colorful trademark toucan. Coincidentally, at about this same time clothing manufacturers in the U.S.A. and Great Britain began to put a small loop at the back of men's and boys' shirts, just below the yoke and at the top of the pleat between the shoulder blades. These loops, of no apparent purpose aside from the decorative, were seen by some as overly affected and perhaps effeminate additions to the garment and thus were dubbed "fruit loops," the implied reference to a street word for homosexual combining with a pun on the recently introduced cereal brand.

Among adolescent boys in the American Midwest in schools somewhat akin to the local *gymnasia*, a sort of game developed in which the object was to sneak up behind one's companion and, with a quick motion, rip the "fruit loop" from the back of his shirt. For the author of these words, nothing evokes the near-frenzied school days of adolescence more vividly than the recollection of snatching at someone's "fruit loop" in a crowded hallway between classes, or of having one's own suddenly and unexpectedly torn off.

Naturally, illegal activity soon followed. In a small-town high school in the Great Lakes region of Ohio, in the spring of 1964, a boy by the name of Jim Robey, while attempting to snatch the "fruit loop" of a boy named Randy Case, happened to tear the other boy's shirt virtually in half from top to bottom. A full-scale fistfight broke out in which most of the eighth-grade boys ended up taking part; the school administration became involved, parents were called in, criminal charges were almost filed, replacement of the shirt was demanded, and bitter resentments lasted even after the Cases had moved to Illinois.

Thankfully, the chances of this happening to you are small. Nowadays, in the widespread euphoria over the rise of free-market economics, the terrors of high school in the past century seem very far away, with good reason. If, however, you are one of those travelers visiting the city as part of a high school tour group, it pays to exercise all the caution you would at home.

On the Boulevard Joe Namath

This lovely wide avenue lined with linden trees, the city's favorite promenade for seeing and being seen, was not originally named for the American professional football star. Someone or other who was king during the Hundred Years' War apparently named it after his son or close friend who was killed in 1346 at the Battle of Crécy. Laid out to form one of the arms of a commemorative Maltese cross (the other three arms were never completed), the avenue quickly attracted the city's most fashionable society and became the scene of many historic events. Pope Anatoly I, "the traveling pope," pitched his papal tent along its upper reaches in 1495; some years later Martin Luther, in an act of defiance, held an eel-pulling on the very spot where the pope had lain. More recently Joe Namath, whose victory over the heavily favored Baltimore Colts (which he himself predicted) in Super Bowl III will never be forgotten, was also here. Enormous banners advertising Namath's appearance in a touring production of *Li'l Abner* at the Mariinsky Theatre stretched high above the street from one side to the other, causing some visitors and tour guides, for convenience' sake, to refer to the boulevard by his name. So cleverly is the city designed that no matter where one sets out from or which direction one follows, one seems always to end up back on this glorious boulevard.

It is here and in similar places, not in airport shuttle buses or in the duty-free shop at the airport, that the true life of the city goes on. Here young couples walk arm in arm in the evening, enjoying each other and the cosmopolitan crowd—priceless entertainment that even the poorest can afford. On the narrow streets feeding into the boulevard, and in its basement cafés, and even on the pedestals of the Art Nouveau sylphs of the apartment facades, the city's inhabitants gather at day's end to socialize. Some are dressed in the height of fashion;

some do not yet know the dangers of mixing stripes and plaids. All are savoring this brief respite in their lives, and their faces alone tell a story more eloquent than any book. A few, indeed, are wearing the distinctive green-and-white jersey of the New York Jets with the number 12, the number Namath always wore. These jerseys, given out perhaps for nothing or at cost to promote the show at the Mariinsky, can provide a lively opportunity for impromptu conversation. Disregarding your lack of knowledge of the language, you might mention to the jersey wearer the outline of Namath's life: how he grew up in the gritty steel town of Beaver Falls, Pennsylvania; how he played college football at Alabama under the great coach Bear Bryant; and how he went on to New York City and the Jets and became "Broadway Joe." Accompanied by appropriate gestures, a few simple phrases can convey a lot.

And above it all the serene, overarching sky, so limpid and infused with light, continues to offer inspiration as it did to poets and painters of old. In its depths you can perhaps see the spires of the ideal city of which the real one surrounding you is merely a magnificent approximation. The towering clouds, like the ones in that Virgin Airways ad, draw the eye ever upward above the rooftops into higher, brighter realms. There is, quite simply, no other city like this in the world. Of course you will come back, perhaps as early as next year, depending on the fares. And if, by some misfortune, you see the city only once, yet you will always keep it with you in memories and photographs. The great Goethe once made a very famous remark about the city. It may be found in almost every book of well-known quotations, cross-referenced under his name. And yet, we feel, even Goethe himself, for all his talent, failed to capture the spirit at the city's heart. It eluded him, as it always, finally, eludes us all. Shimmering beyond the reach of those who seek it, the timeless city remains unknown and uncaptured, waiting for new eyes to discover it with the dawn of every reasonably priced vacation day.

The American Persuasion

Part I: The Scent of Liberty

George Washington dabbed a few drops of fragrance behind his ears and turned from his dressing table to face the handsome Marquis. The question remained unspoken between them, hanging in the candlelight.

"More brandy, General?" The Marquis broke the silence.

"No, thank you. I don't like what it does to my face."

The General looked away again, and made a mouth at himself in the dressing-table mirror. For a long moment, as if he were alone in the room, he studied what he saw there—those remarkable features which, he knew, looked different to each person who saw them. To one observer, he appeared to be a Roman senator in toga and mantle; to another, a rough-hewn American everyman; to another, a fascinating coquette; to another, great Mars himself, indomitable god of war. Since his youth, Washington had understood the power of his beauty, and he was not above using it now.

"But, my dear Monsieur Marquis," he said, in a low and thrilling tone, "you give me no answer to my request!"

The Marquis threw back his head and laughed a long laugh, loud and Gallic. "Ah, you are a persistent minx, my dear

General. What can I do but agree? Yes, very well—I will help you in your 'revolution,' Monsieur Washington, since you are so eager that I do so. Now come here and sit on the divan, and let's have a better look at you."

Subtle, flirtatious, and amusing (as well as honest and upright), George Washington led the colonists' war against the British with all the wiles at his command. Contemporaries marveled at the flexibility of his methods when pursuing a much desired goal. It was perhaps a lucky accident of history that his cause was aided by patriots nearly as nuanced and seductive as he: in Boston were Paul Revere and John Hancock and the Adamses, noted voluptuaries and lovers of pleasure, easily distinguished in a crowd by the rich, ambergris-based New England bath oils in which they drenched themselves. From Virginia came the great planter aristocrats, with their blooded horses and sumptuous homes—statesmen like the elusive Jefferson and the cunning Henry Lee, and James Madison, so lively and changeable he was called the Chameleon. But to their homegrown talents Washington wished to add that skill at maneuvering and intrigue which is distinctively French. Thus, his single-minded courtship of the Marquis, who would one day be known to history as the Revolution's hero, the noble Lafayette.

Indeed, the Frenchman eventually became quite besotted with the American commander, as Washington grew stronger and the balance of power between them shifted. In his journal for November 8, 1779, Lafayette wrote, "At G.W.'s headquarters this morning—left my *carte de visite*. The adjutant, however, told me the General was out. Such trickery! I am certain he was nearby, from the intoxicating aroma of that perfume he always wears. Later I learned he had really been within, conferring with that Pole, Colonel Kościuszko. He is playing the two of us poor foreigners against each other. Even worse, his cruel plan will succeed. Tomorrow I will tell him he can have still more troops, and more louis from my personal fortune, Heaven forgive my soul!"

Often, for consolation, Lafayette turned to Benjamin Franklin, the fabulously wealthy Philadelphian, one of the most skillful backstairs fixers in Revolutionary times. Franklin's bald pate, side hair, and little glasses belied the shrewd and jaded sophisticate behind the mask. Few of his fellow colonists were more comfortable with their sexuality than Franklin was with his. His wide and varied erotic experience gave him much in common with the European nobility with whom he dealt as America's first ambassador; had circumstances been different, he might well have become the leading courtesan of the age. Franklin hated sexual repressiveness of any kind, and also the unfair tax on tea. Following his example, America's fledgling diplomatic corps developed a policy of sexual uninhibitedness and support for democratic principles which would become the hallmark of the new country's foreign relations.

Quaker Moonlight, Franklin's favorite scent, came in a little spray bottle shaped like William Penn and contained a large percentage of animal essences that we now know to be pheromones. All Franklin and his fellow colonists knew was that it worked. When they had a rich arms manufacturer or financier they particularly wanted to impress, they really poured it on, and set the poor man's head aswirl. Some of Franklin's business deals were taught in European universities for years after the Revolutionary War had been won. Eminent statesmen in far-off capitals still blushed when they remembered how the street-smart Pennsylvanian had led them on.

Cajoling, finagling, marching, greasing a few palms, and turning on the charm when necessary, the brave Colonial soldiers gradually overcame the resistance of the British Army. Red-coated regulars who had fought in India and Ireland proved vulnerable to tactics they had never met before. In South Carolina, Francis Marion, the colonists' famed Swamp Fox, filled an opposing general's tent with flowers on the eve of an important battle, and added a flattering note about how handsomely the Englishman sat on his horse; discomfited, though more than a little pleased, the English general did not know what to do, and the next morning withdrew in confusion from the field. Personality and salesmanship were the weapons of choice in northern regions like New Hampshire and Vermont. Ethan Allen and his Green Mountain Boys, for example, had smiles that could absolutely make you melt. Concerned about the large number of loyalists in that region, Ethan Allen's ragtag band of farmers and tradesmen took every one of them to lunch, handed out small gift baskets of toiletries, and were rewarded with a very high rate of conversion. (After the war, however, they hanged every former loyalist they could find.)

Allen and his men wore a perfume they invented themselves, a kind of balsam-juniper-bay-rum thing, which made a strong statement about who they were. Essentially, what it said was "Don't tread on me! Live free or die!" etc.—but not in an off-putting way. Unfortunately, the original recipe has been lost. Allen always emphasized to his soldiers the importance of how they presented themselves.

Indeed, his training was so successful that many of his troops, former mountain hayseeds, were able to get jobs in the public sector after the war. This pattern was repeated among many veterans of the Continental Army, from general down to private. A number of high-ranking officers caught the eye of their British opponents, and obtained lucrative positions in England after they were mustered out. Similarly, many of the rank-and-file soldiers learned skills in the service which made them excellent butlers and footmen and contributed to a sharp postwar drop in the unemployment rolls.

By the end of the Revolutionary War, what we have come to think of as "the American style" had been fully formed. Soon, all the world would know of this new country and of its people, who were like none that had ever been seen before. This newly minted person, the American, was an independent fellow—bold, forthright, deeply aware of how he looked and smelled, and unashamed of his sensuality. He knew his young country didn't have the mightiest army or navy, and yet he bowed down to no one, except in business deals where it was customary and he had to, and he feared, as he put it, "nobody but the loan officer and God." He believed in freedom, wife swapping, couples sex, and the rule of law, and he clearly embodied many of these beliefs in a noble document, the Constitution. He was friendly as could be, and he loved a good party, and the next morning you might wonder what it was he'd sold you a thousand of, but that was just his way.

He didn't care what anybody said or wrote. He didn't care, probably, if you lived or died. But then maybe he'd see a different aspect to you and get to feeling sentimental, and send a package in the mail. He loved the land; no matter whose it was, he loved it all the same. Filled with a restless energy, the American was always moving on, and making sure you did, too. But introduce him to a powerful magnate and offer him regular overtime plus insurance and benefits, and that would definitely get his attention. He knew how to please a boss, and industry flocked to him. But then someday he might buy a lucky lottery ticket and win so much money that he bought out the boss and now everybody had to call *him* boss, and how about that? It happened all the time. In the ceaseless creation and re-creation first set in motion by the savvy Founding Fathers, the churning engine of democracy made the same people wealthy again and again, while the American moved to take his place center stage in world affairs. At last, Washington's lushly perfumed dream was about to unfold.

Techno-Thriller

Opening shot of the Mall in Washington, D.C., seen from above through an office window. Then the focus becomes blurry.

Sound of clicking keys on a computer keyboard.

KEYS: *Click-click-click-click-click. Click-click-click. Click-click-click-click-click-click-click-click-click-click-click.*

(Pause.)

KEYS: *Click-click-click-click. Click. Click.*

The shot moves from the blurry window across a desk to show fingers poised above the computer keyboard. Just the ends of the fingers, not the whole hand. The fingers hover, slightly trembling, indecisive.

Close-up of an almost full cup of coffee next to the computer.

KEYS: *Click-click-click. Click . . . click . . .*

Shot of the fingers moving over the keyboard. Extreme close-up of right index finger moving slowly, slowly, to the Enter key. It pauses above the Enter key for several seconds. Then it hits the key.

Burst of loud, suspenseful music. Sudden close-up shot of computer screen. Flashing, in greenish computer type on the

screen, the words ILLEGAL OPERATION ILLEGAL OP-
ERATION ILLEGAL OPERATION.

An alarm sounds: *Wee-ooo wee-ooo wee-ooo wee-ooo . . .*

Close-up of holes in the computer speaker the alarm is
coming out of. Shot of fingers moving quickly on keyboard.

KEYS: *Click-click! Click-click-click! Click-click-click-click!*

Alarm stops.

Scene 2

Close-up of a satellite in outer space with Earth in the back-
ground. The satellite has radio dishes sticking out on both
sides, antennae, robotic arms, etc.

Close-up of satellite's control panel. A red light on it is
blinking. The red light stops blinking. After a few seconds a
green light goes on.

Scene 3

Shot of same computer as before. Close-up of coffee cup. Now
it is about half full.

KEYS: *Click-click-click-click-click-click-click-click.*

Close-up of computer screen. It is blank. Then moving
geometric patterns appear on it, get smaller, and disappear.
Again the screen is blank.

KEYS (confidently): *Click-click-click-click-click-click.*

More geometric patterns, but different ones this time.
They move faster and vibrate excitedly and disappear. Then,

with a tinkling three-note bell of welcome, the words AC-
CESSING DEFCON CODE FILES pop onto the screen.
Close-up on these words until they're huge.

WHISPERED VOICE: *Bingo!*

Scene 4

Shot of microchip magnified ten thousand times. Sudden
close-up of its circuitry. Burst of scary *whang-ang-ang-ang-ang*
sound.

Scene 7

Shot of space station. It goes by the satellite of Scene 2. Close-
up of satellite. Now many lights are flashing strangely on its
control panel. One of its robotic arms begins to move.

Scene 12

Shot from an office window showing minarets, onion domes,
and other foreign-looking tops of buildings.

Sound of clicking keys. These keys sound different—
sharper, more sinister.

KEYS: *Cleck-cleck-cleck-cleck-cleck-cleck-cleck-cleck.*

Shot of keyboard, with fingers moving on it. They are long
and slender, with manicured red fingernails.

Close-up of computer screen. Jingling tambourine rattle of

welcome as the words FILE ACCESS DEFCON CODING appear. Close-up on these words until they're huge.

WHISPERED VOICE: *Bh'haitvan!*

Scene 19

Shot of big room full of computers with nobody at them. Subtitle says THE PENTAGON. Shot goes unhurriedly along row after row of computer screens, all dark. After many rows it passes a screen on which the words UNAUTHORIZED ENTRY are blinking over and over. It goes back for a close-up on that screen. Somewhere, softly and forebodingly, a military band begins to play.

Shot continues down rest of rows of blank computer screens.

Scene 26

Split-screen shot of keyboards. On left, keyboard from opening scene; on right, keyboard from Scene 12. Ordinary fingers and red-fingernail fingers typing.

KEYS (on left): *Click-click-click-click-click!*

KEYS (on right): *Cleck-cleck-cleck-cleck-cleck!*

Typing goes on getting faster, accompanied by tense music. Scene lasts about half an hour.

Scenes 30–45

Additional plot: shots of computer screens, fingers typing, frantic mouse clicks, tidal wave, explosions, ringing phones, papers pouring from fax machine, beepers going off, etc.

Scene 51

Sudden terrifying shot of computer screen seen from below as if about to fall on you. Symbols flash rapidly across it as sound of typing and mouse clicks becomes deafeningly loud. Nervous music rising.

Jarring full-screen shot of digital clock with glowing red numbers complete to the thousandth of a second. The numbers are moving, going backward to zero. The clock has about fifty-eight seconds on it.

Shot of fingers typing really fast.

KEYS: *Click'ick'ick'ick'ick'ick'ick'ick'ick'ick'ick!*

Alternating shots of clock running down and fingers typing. Music reaches crescendo.

Suddenly clock stops. There are eleven thousandths of a second left.

Scene 55

Shot of Harrison Ford and Julia Roberts embracing.

Scene 58

Shot of satellite. All its robotic arms are retracted. It is orbiting peacefully and looks fine.

Scene 60

Shot of fingers turning off computer. This takes several minutes because of the steps involved. Finally screen goes blank.

Extreme close-up of right index finger moving to turn off little yellow-green light in right-hand corner below computer screen. Tired but relieved, the finger pushes the button. Gradually, the light dims.

Triumphant music as the credits roll.

The Cursing Mommy Cookbook

If you're like me, with a husband and two kids, and nobody ever does anything around the house but you, then quick and tasty dinner recipes are just what you need. With so many demands on your time, you want healthful, attractive, and delicious dinners to set before your family every night as easily as you can—not that they even notice anyway, of course.

Chili, a perennial favorite, can be made in quantity and reheated on subsequent nights, saving you even more effort and time. Here's a chili recipe I've devised with careful thought and much streamlining to be almost trouble-free.

Twenty-Minute Chili
(with Rice and Salad)

Break up a pound and a quarter of lean ground beef and sauté it in a large saucepan. If you have removed the meat from the freezer earlier in the day, it should be defrosted by now. (How come this is still frozen? The goddamn center is still frozen.) If for some goddamn reason the center is still frozen, stick it in the mi-

crowave for thirty seconds or so to thaw. If you don't
have a microwave, break the frozen part into small
pieces with a fork or your fingernails or something before sautéing and it will probably be okay.

A key to the taste of this dish is just the right
amount of onion: too little, and the chili will be bland,
but too much and a cloying sweet taste is the result.
Chop one to two medium onions, not overly fine, and
add to the browning meat. If the onion has some dark
or moldy parts, as this one does (I just bought these
goddamn onions last week, for Christ's sake!), then cut
those parts off and throw them away.

Open one twenty-eight-ounce can of whole peeled
stewed tomatoes and two sixteen-ounce cans of red,
pinto, or kidney beans, if you can get the stupid goddamn electric can opener to work. I like to use two or
more different kinds of beans, for color and variety.
Mix the tomatoes and beans with the sautéed meat and
onions, chopping the stewed tomatoes a bit as you do.

Once all these ingredients are blended together
and simmering nicely, it's time to add the chili powder. Personally, I recommend Durkee brand chili powder,
not too hot and not too mild, with a rich dark color.
(Usually it's right here in the spice rack . . . or maybe
in the cupboard . . . don't tell me we're out of chili
powder! We CAN'T fucking be out of chili powder!
We are! I can't fucking believe it. I fucking forgot to
buy chili powder! Now I have to get in the fucking
goddamn car and go to the goddamn fucking A&P!
Goddamn fucking shit! Why doesn't anybody fucking

tell me when we're fucking out of fucking chili powder? Because nobody lifts a fucking finger around here except me, that's why!)

[Door-slam. Engine noise. Screech of tires.]
[Brief pause.]

Once you have obtained the fucking goddamn chili powder, and once you have removed the useless goddamn fucking plastic seal on the top of the chili powder bottle, add a moderate amount to the simmering ingredients. Season to taste, sampling the chili while adding more powder a little at a time, careful not to burn your . . . FUCK! Seasoning chili is, obviously, a very personal matter, so just put in however the hell much you fucking feel like. As I said, they're probably not going to know the difference anyway.

Make some goddamn rice to go with it. Wash some fucking lettuce. Put it in some salad bowls, or just let them eat it with their hands out of one big bowl. What a fucking terrible day this has been, so don't bother with the goddamn salad dressing. Maybe there's still some Thousand Island in a bottle in the refrigerator somewhere, but who the hell cares?

Serves four, and they'd better fucking like it.

NEXT WEEK: Recipes from the Cursing Mommy's *Cooking with Cat Hair*.

Veni, Vidi, Vici, Etc.

The sound bite, that form of speech we encounter in the media every day, seems a unique contribution of our technological age. Electronic communication, we imagine, has created a new style of utterance as swift, short, and powerful as the electronic impulse itself, stripping away all nonessential sound and meaning. Anyone who has studied history, however, knows that this assumption, apparently self-evident on the face of it, turns out to be very far from the truth. Humans have been abbreviating and editing their remarks almost since the first paleoanthropus opened his mouth. Many of mankind's most profound quotations are actually shortened versions of longer statements compressed into historic sound bites by various forces of their times.

As a scholar whose special field is the work of the French philosopher René Descartes, I first became aware of this phenomenon while looking over some original manuscripts in the Bibliothèque Descartes, in Reims. The most famous quotation of Descartes, as every schoolboy knows, is, of course, *"Je pense, donc je suis"*—"I think, therefore I am." Like many modern students of Descartes, I had met this statement in the philosopher's magisterial *Discours de la Méthode*, in an English translation from the author's edition of 1637. When I examined the corresponding vellum sheets of Descartes's original manuscript in the archives, however, I discovered to my surprise that the great man's initial formulation of his now immortal statement was a bit longer, and certainly more enigmatic, than the quotation we have come to know. In his flowing, feathery script, Descartes had written not "*Je pense, donc je suis*" but "*Je pense, donc je suis Wayne Rogers.*" Descartes always composed a second copy in Latin, so I quickly checked it as well. There I found not the familiar "*Cogito, ergo sum*" but, more problematically, "*Cogito, ergo sum Patrick Duffy.*" A rough translation into English—"I think, therefore I am Paul Reiser"—indicates how different Descartes's original, unedited quotation was.

What to make of this? Did Descartes literally mean to say that by the act of thinking he became Paul Reiser (or, in the French, *Wayne Rogers*)? Basic common sense argues against such a conclusion. In the first place, the popular TV personality of the same name or names would not even be born for another three hundred years. Surely the mention of Paul Reiser was just a fortuitous slip of the pen. And yet, with a mind as subtle as Descartes's, the most unexpected inspiration never can be ruled out. That he wrote "*Cogito, ergo sum Patrick Duffy*" expert handwriting analysis leaves no doubt. He must have meant *something* by it. Whether a later editor shortened the statement, or whether Descartes thought better of the original and made the change himself, or whether the short version was simply the result of a typesetter's error we may never know for sure.

In any event, by the time the quotation was pared down, a lot of richness and shading had been lost. When we examine the famous statements of the great and near-great throughout history, we find that happening again and again. In antiquity, quotations might be cut in order to fit on monuments, and so that they wouldn't take too long to carve. During the age of Julius Caesar, for example, everybody knew he didn't just say, "I came, I saw, I conquered," and leave it at that. A member of Caesar's entourage told a friend, who passed it on to the historian Flavius Josephus, that after winning one of the Gallic wars, Caesar remarked, "*Veni, vidi, vici, edi morsiunculam, balneo usus sum, et cubitum ii, quoniam defatigatus eram.*" ("I came, I saw, I conquered, I had a snack, I took a bath, and I went to bed, because I was exhausted.") The short version of this remark sounds impressive, but it makes him seem rather conceited and cold. When we read the full quotation, we see Caesar as a human being with needs like anybody else.

Often, sycophants and flatterers spruced up the quotations of powerful people in the hope of winning favor; almost every witty comment attributed to a king or queen started out this way. One evening at court, Louis XIV, the redoubtable Sun King, was holding forth on the subject of political power in France, and pronounced, "*L'état, c'est . . . umm . . . l'état, c'est, ahhh, c'est comme une très grande chose . . . umm . . . c'est un petit peu comme un très grand bifteck, ou quelque chose!*" This sally of the king's completely eluded all his listeners, leaving his top aides and ministers in a panic of embarrassment. One of them, covering quickly, began laughing appreciatively, and, when asked what he was laughing about, repeated the king's remark, only much abbreviated and wittier. It got such a warm burst of applause that Louis pretended it was what he'd really said.

War heroes, too, have benefited from the public's desire to keep it short and sweet. John Paul Jones, America's first naval hero, definitely did utter his famous "I have not yet begun to fight!" during a battle with an English ship as the bullets flew. However, on that occasion he also explained why he had not yet begun to fight, said what he was going to do when he did begin to fight, pointed out where he planned to fight, and described how sorry the enemy would be after he finally fought, none of which we really needed to know. Like many sea captains, Jones loved the sound of his own voice, and did not understand that you should put a cork in it once in a while.

From a historical perspective, it was but a short step from Jones's time to the age of modernism, when brevity and starkness of speech became the style. Yet even here we see the sanitizing hand of propriety cutting quotations to make people seem better than they were. The famous writer Gertrude Stein, for one, would have a much worse reputation today if the well-known statements attributed to her had come down to us just as spoken. To cite only one example: Ms. Stein did not say of Oakland, California, "There is no there there." What she actually said was "There is no there there, you stupid idiot." Others of her remarks—"A rose is a rose is a rose, for Chrissake!"—have had to be purged of inappropriate characterizations, personal slurs, and gratuitous profanity.

A mysterious combination of natural forces, it seems, eventually cuts quotations down to a reasonable length and makes them into something that people actually want to hear. But, as we have seen, this can be both a blessing and a curse for mankind. On the positive side, it has freed up large blocks of time, because the human mind can express an infinity of ideas in language of marvelous variety and complexity, which sometimes becomes a real time-waster if it runs on too long. On the very negative side, however, we despair when we think of the many great parts of famous quotations that probably have been lost. Who knows how stirring a declaration like "I only regret that I have but one life to lose for my country" might have been before it got edited down? The missing words of that quotation, if they in fact existed in the first place, are now gone forever.

Sadly, we fail again and again to accept the full truth there before us in what we see or read. Before we can take in another's words, we often mutilate them to fit our own tiny imaginations. For the rest of my professional life, I'm sure I will be haunted by the discovery I made that rainy afternoon in the Descartes archives, when, with heart pounding, I read and reread my translation of his words: "I think, therefore I am Paul Reiser." If only Descartes's contemporaries, or whoever passed the quotation down to posterity, had stepped back, thought twice, and left it exactly as it was! Perhaps then the eminent philosopher and mathematician would be known today as a nearly supernatural prophet as well. "I think, therefore I am Paul Reiser": it's a riddle, an augury, a strange statement of faith, perhaps even a blueprint for a future we have yet to build.

Kidproof

The day I heard that my wife was going to have a baby, I crossed an internal watershed, a kind of Continental Divide of the spirit, and I knew I would never be the same. I was in front of my apartment complex at the time, sitting on the lawn. A guy I used to know from my old job came walking by, and we were talking about one thing and another. Suddenly he happened to ask when Nancy's baby was due. The waves of emotion that rushed over me in that instant are difficult to describe. First, I suppose, was an overwhelming sense of wonder—wonder at the power of life, at its simple, unfathomable glory. Along with that came surprise, as I cast back in my mind for clues I might have missed and tried to recall her present address. Then came pride, and a happiness of a sort I had never felt before, all mixed up with anxiety at this new responsibility that I might possibly have. There was a welter of other feelings as well—financial worry, concern for the legal aspects, puzzlement, excitement, even perhaps a moment of terror at the change I could feel taking place inside me. And through it all, and above it all, that enormous feeling of wonder.

Then I had to laugh. My acquaintance was still standing there talking to me, and here I was a million miles away. I always get a kick out of watching my reaction to things. Right then, I decided to keep a journal, to record my emotional growth through this uncharted new region I had entered in my life.

May 5: A week since I first heard the news, and still I lie awake nights saying to myself, "Me, a father (putatively)!" For hours, as the traffic passes outside, my mind examines the idea from every angle. I mean, the last time I saw Nancy was March, and that's not too long ago, and before that we were pretty much together, so I'd have to say that the chances are fairly good— better than sixty-forty, at least. Only Nancy could truly appreciate my thoughts right now—I must get in touch with her. My search begins no farther away than the kitchen counter, where I file the messages that my landlord has been taking for me while I wait for my dispute with the phone company to be resolved. I am quickly rewarded with a handful of scraps of paper with the words "Call Nancy" and a scrawled number. I recall how in the past I always ignored their summons, fearful of reopening old wounds. Now I stuff the scraps in my jacket pocket and rush to the public phone at the arcade.

A male voice answers—an instructor from Lamaze, almost certainly. Then, after an endless moment, Nancy is on the line. Nancy, my Nancy, my woman, my love, with her heart welling up through the familiar music of her voice. Scarcely able to muster breath, I ask her if it's true that we're going to have a baby. She replies that she definitely is pregnant. The mystery of it all bewitches us for a second or two, making us fall silent. Then, like dams finally giving way, we spill forth a stream of questions. She wants to know why I didn't call her before, and if I have the money I owe her, and what I did with her space heater, and how come I never paid my share of something or other—the usual concerns, but infused with new meaning now. Of course, I respond with dizzy inquiries of my own. Then, again, we both fall silent—she because she has hung up, and I because this idea of my (or somebody's) being a dad will take a little getting used to.

July 15: Rushing around like mad preparing for the new baby. I'm on the go constantly from when I wake up, at about noon, until the dinner hour, or later. Kidproofing my apartment and storage unit was a job that lasted for days. One minute I'm thinking I'd better start using ashtrays, and the next I'm thinking about how to keep them out of tiny hands. I can see how people who are pretty sure they're parents get obsessed with this stuff.

August 9: Pregnancy is a state of mind that affects not just the woman but also the man (assuming I'm him). Along with a powerful nesting impulse that's come over me, I've experienced a change in my diet, accompanied by a craving for strange foods. These days, I have a taste for pickled hard-boiled eggs, hot-pepper vodka, salty beef jerky, sugarcoated peanuts, strong beef bouillon with vodka, pork rinds, Irish coffee, and rich brandy Alexanders—often in odd combinations. Many days, too, I suffer from nausea and other symptoms of sympathetic morning sickness.

September 1: Saw Nancy coming out of a tanning parlor with a guy, very likely her nutritionist. Remembered I've been meaning to call her and catch up. Felt a surge of affection as I waved from the bus.

October 20: I've become very involved in the new fall lineup of shows, on both network and cable. For the first time, however, my loyalty is split. Yes, I want to watch them all, as I've done in the past. But my thoughts keep wandering to this pregnancy, and to the imminence of my probably being a dad. Already I'm evolving into a different person; my viewing schedule will never have my undivided attention again.

November 15: I want to weep, or stick my head out the window and shout for joy. How powerful, how unfamiliar these feelings are! Just now, as I was leafing through the local paper, I saw it in the "Vital Statistics" column: Nancy's name, and the announcement of the birth of her seven-pound-six-ounce baby boy. I have a son (pending DNA testing)!

I made a mental note to call Nancy again, ASAP. Or as soon as she's out of the hospital, anyway, which would probably be next week.

November 23: Although constantly repeated, the miracle of a life coming into the world is always new, a blessing and an astonishment every time. However I had imagined myself feeling, I never imagined this. It's as if someone took out my heart and shined it up and put it back inside me, better than before. I tried to share my revelations with Nancy's brother Rick when he stopped by today. He only wanted to talk about inconsequential financial business involving some car loan in my and Nancy's name that I defaulted on and they froze her checking account and garnisheed her salary. Somehow the issue of x thousand dollars that I may or may not owe seems so meaningless now, especially in light of the wonderful recent events that have happened to me.

November 29: What a pleasure it is to have a baby to shop

for! I'm sure that Nancy's parents and other relatives on her side are buying him many things. As my contribution, I decided to get him a special gift that was just for fun. After much looking, I settled on a small plastic container of anise-flavored toothpicks. He won't appreciate them until he's older, but he'll be glad he has them then. And for myself I splurged on—what else?—a big Costa Rican cigar and a couple of cartons of Pall Malls, since I was at the store anyway.

December 3: Spotted Nancy at a back table at the corner bistro in close confab with a guy—possibly the author and pediatric-medicine expert Dr. T. Berry Brazelton. Wanted to go over and join them, but thought better of the idea. What could I add to their discussion, after all? As the mother, Nancy is far better informed about the baby's medical history than I. The simple fact is, Nancy is the most important person in that kid's world right now, regardless of what I or the actual father, if it isn't me, may feel.

December 11: Among the greatest experiences in a man's life has to be the moment when "his" baby smiles at him for the first time. That epiphany just happened to me, leaving me dazzled, humbled, and in awe. I was in the parking lot at Price Chopper and I saw a baby in an infant-restraining seat in the back of what I took to be Nancy's car. I stopped and admired the child through the window and made a silly face, and there it was—a smile. The child sort of seemed to be smiling and crying simultaneously, if that's possible. I think he has my eyes, or one of them.

December 14: I'm exhausted. The last few nights I've been up at all hours, walking the floor and feeding. I hate to think how much tireder I'd be if I were taking care of a baby. I can tell that this experience is aging me—but in a good way. Early this morning, I was relaxing in a nightspot, and suddenly I couldn't believe the words I heard coming out of my mouth. Turning to the server, I offhandedly remarked, "I'll have one more round, please, and a six-pack to go." As the sentence replayed in my mind, the realization hit me: I sounded just like my own father (or the guy who used to say he was)! Without consciously trying or knowing I was doing it, I had become him, somehow; now the words of that beloved long-dead or moved-away person had been officially handed on to me.

March 12: Had to go to West Virginia for a few months, and so got behind in this. After all I'd been through, I needed to recharge my batteries. I believe that everyone who has the burdens of child care should do the same. You need to make time that's just for you. Stop for a moment, sit down, lean your head back, put a damp washcloth over your eyes, let the problems of the day flow out your limbs, take a bus to Clarksburg, and find an inexpensive motel room. Three or four months later, you'll be back on your feet and ready to go. In my case, I have returned full of eagerness to plunge into domestic duties again. Pretty soon, I definitely will give Nancy a call.

Seventeen years later: Found this notebook while throwing out some junk. Time goes by so quickly! How long ago was it, I wonder, that I saw a smiling baby through a car window and felt the pride of almost-100-percent-certain fatherhood bring tears to my eyes? It could have been an eternity, or just yesterday. Now that baby I admired is a full-grown man with an important job in a factory and a wife and baby and beautiful home, probably, for all I know. Nancy, perhaps now a plump and cheery grandmother, does not live in this town anymore, because I haven't seen her around. People say that the hardest thing to learn with kids and other loved ones is letting go. But, no matter how difficult it may be, still it can be done, as my own example proves.

The Not-So-Public Enemy

Osama bin Laden, the alleged terrorist mastermind, is wanted by the FBI. No surprise there. What did surprise me, however, was to see bin Laden's face on a "Wanted by the FBI" poster on the wall of a post office in North Bergen, New Jersey. Like many of us, when I go to the post office, I always check out the "Wanted" posters. There's something about those grim faces that adds a thrill to the ordinariness of buying stamps or dropping letters in the mail. Bin Laden's photo brought me up short; among the others, he stood out. His neat white turban got my attention, for starters. And below that, the face—rather narrow, smooth, bearded, almost young—looked back at the observer without guile, even affably.

The FBI puts these notices in post offices because it hopes the public will become informed about certain fugitives and perhaps even aid in their capture. Willing to do my part, I studied bin Laden's poster in every detail. I read what he was wanted for: "Murder of U.S. Nationals Outside the U.S.; Conspiracy to Murder U.S. Nationals Outside the U.S.; Attack on a Federal Facility Resulting in Death." Then, his aliases: "Osama bin Muhammad bin Ladin, Shaykh Osama bin Ladin, the

Prince, the Emir, Abu Abdallah, Mujahid Shaykh, Hajj, and the Director." He was born in 1957. The poster does not mention his high school, but he would have been Class of '75. So far he was pretty much as I'd imagined him. When I got to his physical statistics, however, I had to back up and read them again:

Height: 6'4" to 6'6"
Weight: 140 to 160
Build: Thin

Thin? I'll say he's thin. A more accurate description might be "Really, Really Thin." The guy's a beanpole! What the FBI is telling us is that bin Laden might weigh as little as 140 pounds and be as tall as 6 feet 6 inches. Even if he weighs 160 and stands 6'4", he's a string. Let's assume he's somewhere in between—say, 150 pounds and 6 feet 5. A guy like that would have to run around in the shower to get wet! If he drank tomato juice, he'd look like a thermometer! (Insert your own "thin" joke here.) I mean, this is one skinny terrorist. Not to mention tall! Plus you've got six inches of turban on top of that. A note at the bottom of the FBI poster adds, "Walks with a cane." So the picture emerges of a really tall, really skinny young-looking middle-aged guy walking with a cane thinking about ways to blow up lots of U.S. citizens and writing poetry about the bombings (according to the news) after they occur.

Next question: What would he be doing in suburban New Jersey? The FBI clearly believes there's a chance he might be here, and not in his rumored mountain fastnesses in Afghanistan—or else why go to the trouble of putting up the poster?

As I think back, I recall that one or two of the guys who blew up the World Trade Center frequented a house around the corner from where I used to live in Brooklyn. So looking for him in New Jersey isn't completely far-fetched. But hanging out here would be a big mistake on his part, it seems to me. A skinny stick of a guy with a cane and a turban reading a bomb-making manual is going to draw stares. Plus, he would not be by himself; anyone with nicknames like "the Emir" and "the Director" is going to have an entourage. Considering that your average person is not such a long drink of water, the guys around him will probably be a head shorter than he. A group like that would be easy to spot, even among the Jersey commuters at the Port Authority Bus Terminal.

In time, reading the poster again and again, I felt I really got to know this man. It said that he had once been a construction executive—who'd've guessed—and described his complexion, somewhat improbably, as "olive." I had no doubt I could recognize bin Laden on the street. When I saw his name in the newspaper or on TV, I felt a small tingle of familiarity, as if he were a distant acquintance or a person from my old hometown. You would think that a supposed public enemy of bin Laden's stature would have his "Wanted" poster displayed everywhere, but strangely, I never saw it anyplace but that one post office. Stranger still, when I went to other post offices, I noticed that some had no "Wanted" posters on display at all. Indeed, the "Wanted" poster, as a post office fixture, suddenly seemed to be disappearing under my nose.

First it was the main post office in Montclair, New Jersey—one day it had a large gallery of alleged rogues behind a glass frame by the door; the next, the whole display, frame and all, had vanished with no trace. Another post office I often go to in the same town used to have a handy clipboard with a big selection of "Wanted" posters hanging from a pillar right next to where you stand in line. One day I turned to it, hoping to pass a few minutes of waiting time, and the clipboard wasn't there. I asked the retail associate (the post office no longer uses the word "clerk") behind the counter, and she told me the postmaster had recently received a directive ordering that all "Wanted" posters be taken down.

She gave me the number of the district official of the post office from whom the directive had come. I called him at the district headquarters in Newark—his name is Dominick Balestro and his title is retail specialist. Dominick Balestro said, "Yes, those 'Wanted' posters will no longer be on display. They'll be available behind the counter to customers who request them, but they won't be plastered all over the place like they were before. At the post office we're trying to create a retail environment pleasing to the eye, and those 'Wanted' posters are not pretty pictures. They're not the image of the post office we want our customers to have. We want a bright, positive, clutter-free lobby to advertise our products and services."

Mr. Balestro had himself received a directive on the subject from Gloria Cheek, on the staff of the retail marketing group at U.S. Postal Service headquarters in Washington, D.C. I called her, and she said that removing the "Wanted" posters from display in all lobbies is the post office's national policy, and it's not new. It has been in effect since 1992. She said that any post office that displays "Wanted" posters (except for one or two having to do with postal crimes) is in violation of that policy, and eventually will have to comply, although she understands that old habits die hard. She said that in the past the post office was practically the only place where people looking for information about criminals could see those notices, but nowadays there are other venues, such as *America's Most Wanted* on TV.

Gloria Cheek said that studies have shown that the average customer can take in only four or five messages in a retail environment, and that the old post office lobby, with its army recruitment ads and "Wanted" posters and Selective Service notices, was too confusing. The Postal Service wants to give its customers clarity of message and access to information in a clean retail space similar to that provided by its competitors in the mail- and package-delivery business. People who specifically need to look at the "Wanted" posters—law-enforcement officers and bounty hunters, for example—will still be able to see them by asking at the counter. Nostalgia for the past is fine, she said, but the post office is concerned with providing customers the modern retail services they desire. "We can't do everything we used to do. We add new services and we have to shed old ones. We can't be buggy-whip manufacturers," Gloria Cheek said.

I tried to explain to Gloria Cheek my fascination with the bin Laden poster, but I sounded feckless and hesitant, like a ten-year-old talking about a really neat tree fort he planned to build. Her no-nonsense silence daunted me, and my voice trailed away. This happens to me often when I talk to grown-ups older or younger than I. In the face of arguments invoking efficiency, fairness, and getting with the program, I crumble every time. Of course it's good that the post office wants to be more efficient; no one dislikes standing in line more than I do.

And what is gained, in the end, by idling over a "Wanted" poster for bin Laden, daydreaming about meeting up with him at the A&P? The proper time and place for such fantasies is while watching *America's Most Wanted* in your own home, along with the rest of the country. At the post office from now on I will enter the retail environment, take in its four or five messages, do my errands, and be on my way. Thinking about bin Laden doesn't get my letters mailed. It's not my business to think about the guy.

(Originally published in Mother Jones *magazine, July–August 2001.)*

Unbowed

Russell Crowe, the tough-guy, says the WTC disaster made him blink. "I almost feel like retreating to my ranch in Australia. I guess that would be prudent. But I can't bring myself to hide from this. I'm going about my business, mate. I won't let these bastards affect my life, threat or no threat."

—Liz Smith, *New York Post*, September 25, 2001

Russell Crowe's pastoral life on the Aussie range turned scary recently when a herd of cattle charged him. The actor was fixing fences with his ranch hands when his herd stampeded, according to reports from Down Under. Crowe was knocked down by a steer but came away unscathed.

—Rush & Molloy, *Daily News*, November 26, 2001

Russell Crowe, the human, is going on with his life, according to publicity sources. Spitting defiance, the popular *anthropos* vowed not to be intimidated despite recent scares. "Sure, I could sit up on the porch all day, which is screened in and has a door that they don't know how to open, the bastards," Crowe said. "And, yes, I'll admit that they got my attention with the noise they make, and the way they look at you, and all that slobbering. And if anybody tells you they can't run fast, don't you believe it. Most blokes would take one look and retreat to the equipment shed or climb on top of the pickup. But I couldn't live with myself if I did that."

Crowe emphasizes that he has nothing against ruminants as a whole—he lives and works with them every day. "Look, mate," he explains. "How many stomachs you have, how many times you chew your sodding breakfast—that's completely up to you, far as I'm concerned. You can have fifty stomachs, for all I care. Now, it just so happens that I'm a hominid, with one stomach, one set of teeth, and when I eat something, down it goes and goodbye. That's just who I am. I'm bipedal, too, and proud of it. But I'm not going to go round telling you that mine is the only way, so long as you don't start pushing any of your narrow-minded quadrupedalism on me."

Word in the outback says that Crowe's own species is also unique in its use of language, an accomplishment that's never mentioned by the down-to-earth Aussie star, who forgoes any VIP treatment. In fact, he has always tried to blend in easily with the ranch's ungulates, which makes some of their recent behavior toward him harder to understand. Latest reports indicate that sympathies in the entertainment community are running strongly in Crowe's favor. "I've worked with all the big names—Elsie, Elmer, Ferdinand," one director says. "I can tell you that Russell is a prince compared with them. For one thing, I never have to haze him onto the set in the morning, or wave my hat and flap my arms and yell 'Hsst! Git along!' just so he'll leave his trailer. There's no way in the world he deserved to have this happen."

Pastureland opinion has been more guarded. While silently admiring technological advantages made possible by Crowe's opposable thumbs, many of the ranch's inhabitants blow air from their nostrils in what appears to be anger when he is late to feed them their hay. In addition, the expression on their faces seems to reveal a general distrust of Western methods, such as spraying them with fly-tox when most would prefer the traditional practice of standing front to back and swatting one another in the head with their tails. For many, low standards of education are also a problem: ask even a basic question on the difference between Russell Crowe, Cameron Crowe, and James Cameron and the reply is likely to be a blank stare. Here, as in a number of areas, large cultural gaps remain.

Combat veterinarians with years of experience in the field say that real progress will take time. The first thing Crowe and his ranch hands should do, experts agree, is be careful about flaunting the color red, which some here consider blasphemous, even a provocation. Merely wearing red long underwear can be hazardous, if, for example, your trousers fall down and you bend over to pick them up while in a busy part of the range. Insiders caution that a certain kind of bright red long johns with a buttoned drop seat should be avoided above all. Among a population whose only adornment is tags in their ears, such a display is viewed with blood-maddened eyes, pawing of the earth, and other warning signs. In a few instances, it has even led to skirmishes strikingly similar to the one in which Crowe was involved.

The larger situation is, of course, far more complicated than authorities among the higher primates are letting on. Hollywood sources ascribe the controversy to the old studio system, the discovery of fire, and the making of simple instruments and tools, which led to cranial enlargement and other perks that species not as blessed don't qualify for or understand. Add to this the fact that film stars don't put on weight as efficiently per pound of feed and you can begin to see the dilemma. Clearly, there are going to be trade-offs either way. What's needed is a visionary who can resolve disputes between dairy and non-, leather and Naugahyde, Hereford and Angus, and so on, some of which go back to man's earliest domestication of livestock in the films of Cecil B. DeMille, many years ago. If negotiations are to work under these circumstances, they must include not only the members of *Homo sapiens* but those they milk and barbecue.

For now, Crowe is dusting himself off, brushing away the bits of grass and duff, and planning what he'll do next. "I was unscathed, sport, which means they didn't scathe me," said Crowe in a recent interview. "They want to see scathing, I'll scathe them, you'll see. Listen, George, or whatever your name is, you walk upright, right? Good man—that makes two of us. Now, look, I'm gonna get in this suit, with the head part and horns, see, on me, and this back part here, with the tail, on you. Go ahead, get in. Now we hook it together in the middle here—can you hear me?—and when I say 'Step,' you step with your right leg, and I'll step with my right leg, that's it, now left leg, step, that's the idea. Off we go. They won't know what hit 'em. One thing you can count on with these bastards, they never use their brains."

The New Poetry

The twentieth century began, as we know, not at its calendar date but some years later, perhaps with the sinking of the unsinkable *Titanic* in 1912, certainly with the opening salvo of Allied guns in 1914 announcing the dreadful slaughter they called the Great War. In poetry, however, the new age that would bring such wonders and horrors announced itself rather more promptly, when the novelist turned poet Thomas Hardy informed his still innocent readers:

> The land's sharp features seem'd to be
> The Century's corpse outleant,
> That booty-licious booty there,
> Show 'em what you're workin' with!

Perhaps only a writer whose original vessel was prose would have dared be so straightforward when he added, in verses that millions would eventually know by heart:

> At once a voice arose among
> The bleak twigs overhead

In a full-hearted evensong
Of joy illimited;
Hunh! Hotpants!

Directness of expression, no waste of words, short and lap-
idary lines, a willingness to lapse into vers libre with bursts of
pure feeling—these were the principles of the new poetry that
would take root and spread in the years to come. Many would
be its devotees. The young American Ezra Pound, arrived in
Paris in 1920 with his huge 'fro and obnoxious square shades,
must at first have seemed an unlikely candidate as the movement's chief explainer and impresario. And yet that is exactly
what he became. The poetic ethos sketched in by Hardy ap-
pealed enormously to Pound, whose raw American back-
ground had included a lot of time living on the streets or in
jail. Pound also understood instinctively the generation shaped
by the war.

Pound loved cars, women, and pit bulls. He preferred the
first fast, the second fly, and the third "monster-maulin' and
mean." To a London critic's claim (in *The Transatlantic Review*)
that the poet must serve the spiritual needs of society above
all else, Pound responded with scorn in his widely quoted es-
say "The Lyric Impulse / X-ta-see and Po-a-tree." Money, in
Pound's view, was the poet's primary muse as well as his re-
ward. True to this philosophy, he carried a large bankroll at all
times. Specially inset diamonds, emeralds, and rubies gleamed
from his teeth when he declaimed his verses, and he even had a
Parisian jeweler make a solid-gold laurel wreath for him, which
he wore about his temples when he attended award ceremonies

of the French Academy. Accompanied by his companion Olga Rudge in a backless, almost see-through gown, Pound dazzled onlookers with the insurgent power of modernism.

Nor was Rudge (as it happened) the only big-leg girl in Pound's entourage. Many other poetry-loving ladies of the time had recently come to terms with the extra-large size of their beautiful figures, and weren't shy about saying so. H.D. (Hilda Doolittle), who had been a professional wrestler, made sure that readers knew she did not fit the traditional mold of the wispy, ethereal poetess. Replying angrily to what she took as a slight in Edwin Markham's "The Man with the Ho'," Doolittle signified in blazing verses of her own:

> Thou has flayed us with thy blossoms;
> Spare us the beauty
> Of fruit-trees,
> Chump!
> . . .
> Pomegranates already broken,
> And shrunken fig,
> And quinces untouched,
> I bring thee as offering,
> Suckah!

H.D.'s first collection, *Booty Call*, featured a striking author photo and sold more than a million copies. Her French publisher, Sylvia Beach, considered these numbers very respectable, given the difficulty of the work, and offered a contract for several more volumes. H.D.'s bold eroticism, not to mention her sales, inspired increasingly daring poems by many of her contemporaries, D. H. Lawrence chief among them. Lawrence had been itching to break free from the dead hand of Victorianism, which held the London club scene in its grip even after the war. With a single stroke, Lawrence outraged critics, the public, and the Archbishop of Canterbury when he penned his splendidly transgressive "Thong Song." That work, in particular, marked a point of reference for what was to come; English-language verse was never the same after "Thong Song." Yet in later years Lawrence would partly regret his youthful impetuousness, noting ruefully that, despite his large and distinguished body of writing in many genres, he would always be known as "the 'Thong Song' guy."

It pained him, too, when parents accused him of glamorizing the poetic lifestyle. Neither he nor Pound nor T. S. Eliot, nor any other major writer of their generation, ever set out to do that. In fact, throughout their work they all tried to include messages that made precisely the opposite point. Yes, the sensibility behind a T. S. Eliot poem (for example) might appear elevated and detached among the plentiful absurdities of the modern world; and, yes, that sensibility had an outlaw glamour that might lead young people astray. But always in the last stanza such experienced writers wisely showed the detached poetic sensibility brought low—slapped in handcuffs and thrown in the back of a squad car, or lying dead and full of bullet holes. In truth, these poets could not do otherwise, having been in the "hard-knock life" themselves.

One young mind they surely influenced was that of W. H. Auden, a poetry-besotted undergraduate at Oxford with his own dreams of big-time notoriety. Distaste for confessional writing, which constrained even the most avant-garde of his elders, meant nothing to an up-and-comer like him. Using the first-person singular without hesitation, he introduced to poetry a voice that was intimate, revealing, and completely natural—as in these famous lines written in his early thirties, soon after his arrival in America:

> I sit in one of the dives
> On Fifty-second Street;
> I am a sex machine
> And I'm super bad.
> As the clever hopes expire
> Of a low dishonest decade,
> You gotta get up,
> Now get back. Good God.

Along with this naturalness of diction came an un-aloof readiness to comment on the political situations of the day:

> I and the public know
> What all schoolchildren learn:
> Get up off of that thing,
> And shake, and you'll feel better.

Other Auden works dispensed with narrative and argument entirely, relying instead upon incantatory rhythms reminiscent of medieval mystery plays. For example, his "Ten Songs in Praise of Yo' Booty" used the evocative phrase "Gettin' jiggy wit' it," in multiple repetitions, line after line and, indeed, page after page. Only by such iteration, Auden believed, could the poet convey man's transience in the endlessness of time.

In his personal life, Auden was Peck's Bad Boy, in and out of trouble with the law. His sad, gentle eyes and seamed face gave no indication of the trouble in store if you messed with him. His mother, who supported him throughout his career, always said that the literary rivals Auden shot would have done the same to him if he had given them the chance. Certainly, there was some truth in that. Auden himself blamed his legal difficulties on his fame, and on minor poets and other scribblers who wanted to hang out with him and whom he didn't even know. When a dispute over the acceptability of an off-rhyme led to gunplay, Auden was always the one authorities came looking for.

Time, in its usual fashion, has had the last word. The bitter controversies that once surrounded the new poetry and its champions have faded from memory. Indulgent biographers assure us that we may overlook these poets' occasional bad language, violence, and crimes. They point to the efforts that some of the poets made to reform—to Eliot's later years as a Pentecostal minister, or Lawrence's novellas urging kids to stay in school, or H.D.'s friendship with Mrs. Roosevelt. Unfairly, perhaps, posterity has forgotten sins and virtues alike. It forgets all—all but the poems themselves. The poems remain, along with some incredible film footage, to remind us of when the new poetry broke the rules.

Researchers Say

According to a study just released by scientists at Duke University, life is too hard. Although their findings mainly concern life as experienced by human beings, the study also applies to other animate forms, the scientists claim. Years of tests, experiments, and complex computer simulations now provide solid statistical evidence in support of old folk sayings that described life as "a vale of sorrows," "a woeful trial," "a kick in the teeth," "not worth living," and so on. Like much common wisdom, these sayings turn out to contain more than a little truth.

Authors of the twelve-hundred-page study were hesitant to single out any particular factors responsible for making life tough. A surprise, they say, is that they found so many. Before the study was undertaken, researchers had assumed, by positive logic, that life could not be *that* bad. As the data accumulated, however, they provided incontrovertible proof that life is actually worse than most living things can stand. Human endurance equals just a tiny fraction of what it should be, given everything it must put up with. In a personal note in the afterword, researchers stated that, statistically speaking, life is "just too much," and as yet they have no plausible theory how anyone gets through it at all.

A major disadvantage to living which the study called attention to is, of course, death. In fact, so obvious are its drawbacks that no one before had thought to examine or measure them empirically. Death's effects on life, the scientists pointed out, are two: First, death intrudes constantly and unpleasantly by putting life at risk at every stage, from infancy through advanced adulthood, degrading its quality and compromising happiness. For individuals of every species, death represents a chronic, worrisome threat that they can never completely ignore.

Second, and far worse, death also constitutes an overwhelmingly no-win experience in itself. Many of life's well-known stress producers—divorce, loss of employment, moving, even fighting traffic—still hold out hope of a better outcome in the future. After all, one may end up with a better spouse, exciting new job, beautiful home, or fresh bottle from the drive-through liquor store. Death, by contrast, involves as much trouble as any conventional stress, if not more. Yet, at the end of the medical humiliations, physical suffering, money concerns, fear, and tedium of dying, one has no outcome to look forward to except being dead. This alone, the study found, is enough to give the entire life process a negative tinge.

Besides dying, life is burdened with countless occurrences that are almost equally unacceptable to active and vital individuals. In many cases which the scientists observed, humans no longer functioned properly after the age of seventy or seventy-five. A large majority of subjects in that age range exhibited significant loss of foot speed, upper-body strength, reflexes, hair, and altitude of vertical leap. Accompanying these impairments were other health glitches, sometimes in baffling number and variety. Such acquired traits carried the additional downside of making their possessors either "undesirable" or "very undesirable" to members of the opposite sex in the key eighteen-to-thirty-five demographic. Researchers were able to offer no credible hope for the development of treatments to deal with these creeping inadequacies.

Somewhat simplifying the study's collection of data was the natural law first discovered by Newton that things are rough all over. Thus, what happens to you will always be just as bad (relatively speaking) as what happens to anybody else. Or, to frame it another way, no problem is effectively "minor" if you yourself have it. One example is the mattress cover, or quilted pad, that goes over the mattress before you put on the fitted sheet, and that pops loose from one corner of the mattress in the middle of the night nearly 60 percent of the time, experts say. After it does, it will often work its way diagonally down the bed, taking the fitted sheet with it, until it becomes a bunched-together ridge of cloth poking up at about kidney level. The problem it represents to the individual experiencing it at that moment is absolute, in the sense that it cannot usefully be compared with difficulties in the lives of people in China or anywhere. The poke in the kidneys and the press of bare mattress against the face are simply the accumulating misery of life making itself known.

Nine out of ten of the respondents, identified by just their first initials for the purpose of the survey, stated that they would give up completely if they knew how. The remainder also didn't see the point of going on any longer but still clung to a slight hope for something in the mail. Quitting the struggle and lying facedown on the floor was a coping strategy favored by most or all. Situations like having to wait an entire day for a deliveryman to deliver a breakfront and the guy didn't say exactly when he would be there and in the end didn't come and didn't even bother to call were so pointless and awful that the hell with the whole deal, many respondents said.

Interestingly, the numbers bear them out. The point, or points, of going on with existence, when charted and quantified, paint a very grim picture indeed. Merely trying to get a shoe off a child has been shown to release a certain chemical into the system which causes a reaction exactly opposite to what the task requires. Despite vigorous effort and shouting, the thing won't come off, for Christ's sake, as can be seen in the formula written out in full in Figure 7. Furthermore, that level of suffering doesn't include the additional fact that a person's spouse may not consider what the person does every day to be "work," because he or she happens occasionally to enjoy it; so what is he or she supposed to do, get a job he or she hates, instead? From a mathematical standpoint, this particular problem is an infinite regression.

Flammia Brothers Pharmaceuticals, which paid somebody to say it paid for the study, frankly admits that it does not as yet have the answers. In the interim, it offers a wide array of experience-blocking drugs, which consist of copyrighted names without pills to go with them, and which certainly might work, depending on one's susceptibility, financial history, and similar factors. Hundreds of thousands of notepads with the Flammia Brothers' logo and colorful drug names at the top of every page are already in circulation in doctors' offices and examining rooms, and a soothing poultice may be made of these pages soaked in water and driveway salt from Ace Hardware. (Most health-insurance plans may or may not cover the cost of the salt, excluding delivery.)

Other large drug manufacturers, while not willing to go quite as far, still substantially follow the Flammia Brothers program. The fact that life is beyond us has been firmly established by now. All the information is in, and no real dispute remains. But with the temporary absence of lasting remedies, and looking to a future when they won't be necessary, the manufacturers' consortium suggests that consumers send them money in cash or check, no questions asked. Major health organizations have unanimously endorsed this goal. Originally, the consortium explained that the companies might need the money to develop a new generation of drugs narrowly focused on curing many previously uncured problems. More recently, however, they have backed off of that.

Why we were brought into the world in the first place only to suffer and die is an area of research in which much remains to be done. Like other problems thought impossible in the past, this one, too, will someday be solved. Then anybody afflicted with questions like "Why me?" "What did I do to deserve this?" "How did I get in this lousy mess?" and so on could be given a prescription, maybe even through diagnostic services provided online. The possibilities are exciting. At the same time, we must not underestimate our adversary, life itself. Uncomfortable even at good moments, difficult and unfair usually, and a complete nightmare much too often, life will stubbornly resist betterment, always finding new ways of being more than we can stand.

Warmer, Warmer

President Bush has called for a decade of research before anything beyond voluntary measures is used to stem tailpipe and smokestack emissions of heat-trapping gases that scientists say are contributing to global warming. "When you're speeding down the road in your car, if you've got to turn around and go the other direction, the first thing is to slow down, then stop, then turn," said David K. Garman, the assistant secretary of energy for energy efficiency and renewable energy.

—*The New York Times,*
December 3, 2002

President Bush has called for a decade of additional research on global warming, but needs more time to decide which decade it will be, assistants to the president announced today. So far, 2060–2070 "looks nice," said one insider, though other decades have not been ruled out. "We don't want to pick just any old decade," the source continued, perspiration beading on his forehead. "Finding just the right decade for this type of in-depth climate research might take as long as ten years."

Privately the White House expressed regret that the decade from 1790 to 1800 is past, and thus not able to be a part of their plans. In other respects, it would be an ideal decade for the purposes of research into climate change. Most of the Founding Fathers were still alive then, and with the Revolutionary War over and much of the work on the U.S. Constitution completed, they had free time. The thought of all that talent being brought to bear on the problem is indeed intriguing, as the White House likes to remind critics. President Bush himself is known to have a special fondness for many of the years between 1790 and 1800, particularly 1797, and he has asked his tech staff if anything can be done to get us there. Advances in time travel, or at least in movies about time travel, offer some possibilities, but for now those solutions aren't feasible for political reasons. Inquiries on this subject went unanswered by the White House press office, which had closed early in the February heat.

Other members of the Bush administration who have the president's ear on energy matters refused to give out any information, including where the ear is kept when not in use. They have argued, so far successfully, that that is nobody's business, not even their own. In several recent off-the-record interviews they told the media that an excellent job is being done on national energy policy, now go away. Someone who sometimes delivers their take-out barbecue says he's seen them working really hard, but adds, "Who can formulate policy, or even think, when it's s'dang hot like it's been?" According to an individual who knows this delivery person, he believes the whole process of deciding when we might want to start thinking about global warming would function better if we didn't rush around so, but just laid out by the pool and let the ideas come.

For the moment, the administration seems to agree. Simply letting yourself relax and drill for a while in the Arctic National Wildlife Refuge is a problem-solving technique which, though counterintuitive, may produce surprising results. Similarly, when you ease clean air and water standards, often your whole mind and body ease along with them, allowing access to undreamed-of inner resources of decision making. Loosing some of the bonds of the Endangered Species Act, saying yes to the deeper self that wants to log, letting go of rigid, controlling attitudes toward federal lands—all these, creativity consultants teach, help to free the executive-branch imagination. Of course, mastering mental powers in this way is not done overnight. When it is complete, however, White House staffers promise that the issue of possible global warming will be fully gotten to the bottom of at last.

One proponent of such innovative thinking is David K. Garman, the assistant energy secretary of energy for energy efficiency and renewable-energy energy, with the Department of Energy. Using the new idea-generating method, sometimes called the Halliburton Method, Mr. Garman produced a metaphor, and he held an informal press briefing to share it with reporters. "Okay, say you've got a car," Mr. Garman began, "or no, not just a car—say you've got a really *big* car. Are you with me? Okay, you've got a great big car. You decide to go for a drive. First thing, you go to the convenience store and fill that car up—top your tank right off. Maybe you even bring along a few extra tanks, the ones for the dirt bike and the lawn mower and the chain saw, fill them up, too, because you never know. Then you buy a few snacks, and you're ready. You're heading right straight down that highway—can you all please excuse me for a moment while I change my shirt?"

A complete transcript of Mr. Garman's metaphor was made available after the briefing. Interpreters of figurative language have since examined the metaphor, and they now believe they know what it means. The car, they say, is America, and the driver, responsible businesspeople involved in its governance and energy extraction. The "crybabies in the backseat" are the majority of everybody else in the world. The driver firmly resists their pleas to turn around or even stop for a minute at a restroom (the Kyoto Protocol) until he is good and ready and feels it is in the best interest of the entire car. The "tantrums and whinings" that the driver ignores represent low approval ratings on this one minor isolated topic, and the happy arrival at the driver's destination equals prosperity and peace everywhere.

That this was in fact Mr. Garman's meaning White House sources would neither confirm nor deny. The assistant secretary himself, having left town until the weather breaks, could not be reached. EPA officials running out the door to beat the traffic would say only that whatever Mr. Garman or his friends wanted was all right with them. White House press secretary Ari Fleischer limited his response to blowing through his lips, whinnying, and repeatedly stomping his front foot on the floor as part of a new administration effort to communicate better with the American people by means of friendly sounds. Pressed further, however, Mr. Fleischer said it would be wrong for him to comment beyond the noises he'd just made. Some Beltway observers believe that the administration is hoping the recent news stories of weird savanna wildlife turning up in the suburban Northeast will distract national attention from complicated, wonkish subjects like climate change.

Clearly, it is time for the discussion to move on. "Junk science," as administration sources label much of the data on global warming, has already led many astray. Most laypeople do not understand that higher temperature numbers, in themselves, are not strictly scientific, because they don't use test tubes, Bunsen burners, white smocks, and other equipment familiar from high school science labs. On the contrary, in the real world, hotter weather may be experienced very differently depending on a person's metabolism and daytime job. It is stifling, as we know, in any office when the air-conditioning breaks down. But to employees in a cool and pleasant work space, the same external temperature may appear completely comfortable. So-called climate experts overlook this disparity when they talk about glaciers melting, coral reefs dying, Venice going underwater, etc. Such evidence, while interesting, is not practical science.

One of these days the decade specifically set aside to look into allegations of climate change will arrive. Most of us will not be around then, so dealing with the situation, if there is one, will be up to someone else. If the Bush team has played its cards right, either the people alive then will have gotten to like year-round T-shirt weather, or else the climate will not have changed that much and there was nothing to worry about after all. Or maybe (as is more probable) they still won't know for sure what's going on, but with technology developed in the meantime they will be able to air-condition a much wider section of the planet. And on the remote chance that it really does become a lot hotter, and certain unforeseeable consequences are the result, perhaps they will do as those long before them, and resolve not to think about the problem just now.

A Cursing Mommy Christmas

Holiday festivities are a wonderful way to bring family and friends together. Our seasonal traditions take on a life of their own as the holidays roll round, we find, and all goes as smoothly as can be expected with a little preparation in advance. Details others may not notice (and believe me, they don't) make the season shine. First in importance, of course, is the Christmas tree. I am not sure why, but I've always gotten a real tree, instead of an artificial one, which would probably be much easier. This year, as always, putting up the tree and decorating it, as I'm doing today, marks the official start of the holidays.

First, to set the mood, I put on my favorite tape of Christmas carols, if I can find it. It used to be in this rack here, which I really have to go through and straighten out someday. Okay, thank God, here it is—Nat King Cole. Nobody ever sang "O Holy Night" better than Nat King Cole. With the music playing, and drink in hand, I begin with step one, which is clamping the base of the tree trunk to the surprisingly complicated three-legged holder thing. Okay, I need two hands. The four bolts, minus the one that fell down the stupid heating grate last year, hold the trunk in place when screwed firmly into the rather sticky bark. The kids were supposed to help with this. Now reach through the prickly needles, take hold of the trunk near the top, and stand the tree—ouch! goddamn!—in the desired corner of your den or living room.

I said stand, you goddamn thing. Sometimes you may have to lean the tree a little bit against the wall. Once it is upright, open the wonderful treasure boxes of decorations . . . fuck these lights are a mess. Who put these away last year? Plugging them in first, to make sure they work . . . I can't believe it. Fuck. What the fuck is wrong with these fucking goddamn lights? Why the—

Larry! Larry! These fucking goddamn Christmas lights don't work! Can you hear me? . . . I can't fucking believe it. I'm here all by myself. I'm expected to do this whole fucking job by myself. Fucking typical. Do any of these goddamn lights work?

> *[Interlude of plugging, unplugging, and cursing.]*
> *[Sound of back door slamming. Further interlude of*
>   *about an hour and a half.]*

Once you have purchased several new sets of Christmas lights and have thrown the lousy piece of shit useless former Christmas lights the hell away, you are ready to begin decorating the tree. String the lights on the branches however the hell you want. Ideally, their festive, brightly colored sparkling should cover the entire tree, not just one side, but when the tree must lean against the wall, as is the case here, then fuck that. From a special corner in the decorations box, remove the protective tissue-paper wrapping of all the carefully preserved ornaments made by the children back when they were in elementary school, not that they give a good goddamn about them anymore, and hang the ornaments prominently in places of honor on the tree. Around them distribute the even more delicate ornaments saved from your own and your siblings' childhood, reminders of family Christmases long past.

Speaking of family, you'll want to spread a clean white bedsheet around the base of the tree for that "White Christmas" effect, so each different family group will have a special place to pile its presents when the whole clan assembles on Christmas Eve. But then, on the other hand, why the hell bother? Let them bring their own goddamn sheets. And why the hell do they always have to get together at my house every year? Why am I always the one who has to do all the Christmas bullshit? I notice my sister hasn't done it since . . . God knows when. And my stepmom—don't even ask about her. Bunch of fucking lazy bums, have a good time and go home, leave me to clean up until four in the fucking—

OH, NO! Get the hell off there, you goddamn cats! Don't chase each other up the goddamn tree! Get down, you horrible fucking goddamn animals! You'll fucking knock the goddamn thing—

> *[Crash. Sound of glass splintering, cats screaming, light-bulbs popping.]*
> *[Long interlude.]*

After you've swept up the whole goddamn fucking nightmare mess, tossed it in the trash, thrown the cats out in the yard, and securely duct-taped the top of the tree to the window frame, you deserve a little rest and relaxation. To stay in the spirit, I recommend a seasonal cocktail, like the Happy Holidays Eggnog (*The Cursing Mommy Cookbook*, p. 117). If you happen not to have any eggnog, brandy, or finely chopped nutmeg, a simple glass of pure grain alcohol and tap water will do fine. Taking a sip as you lean back on the couch, you may regard your day's accomplishments with justifiable pride. Remember, however, that Christmas isn't just its material side. What the fuck am I saying? Of course it is. And yet, if on occasion you look inward, as I do, I think you'll discover that the carols of Nat King Cole sound even better when heard for the fortieth time.

> Those interested in other Cursing Mommy publications may wish to order *The Cursing Mommy Fix-It Book, The Cursing Mommy's Guide to Suburban Driving,* or her local bestseller, *Get Your Own Goddamn Lunch: Parenting Tips from the Cursing Mommy,* all soon to be available in paperback from RBS Press.

Come Back, Suckers!

W hat we said was true. You have to admit that. You got mad about it, when all we were telling you was the facts. We very much regret that you took what we said in the manner that you did. But let's have a little acceptance of responsibility here—if you invest in a company that goes bust and you lose your money, whose fault is that? The investor's fault: your fault. The loyal employees of YessCo who put all their money in YessCo stocks, what were they thinking? *Were* they thinking? People like that, of course they're going to get robbed. Did they sniff around, read some interoffice e-mail, ask a few questions about why the bosses were dumping stock? Did they even try to find *out* the bosses were dumping stock? They did not. So they lost everything they had. These folks were not on the ball.

It takes two to make a pump-and-dump stock scheme, don't forget. It takes an ordinary person who wants to get some money and a fool willing to lose it. Sorry—an *investor*, like yourself. But hey, when you play, play to win. Find out who's making calls to his broker from his jet; detect by your own native street smarts which financial analyst whose high-paying job it is to tell you the truth is actually lying to you. Measure the stress level in his voice on the telephone with a common device you can buy in any surveillance-equipment store. Use plain old common sense. We don't have to paint you a picture. If you don't keep these people honest by knowing the same information they know and tracking them every minute, they're going to get away with what they can. They're gonna rip you off, if you let 'em. And . . . what can we say. *You let 'em.* We apologize if this truth is painful for you.

The market's a self-correcting situation, you see, and you're the one who self-corrects it. If you watch these people, then you can invest *smart.* Invest in a company on the basis of what a company says? What dummy would do that? Of course they'll *say* anything.

We're talking about only a few bad apples (as we call them), anyway. No more than five or seven, or maybe three dozen, that flat-out want to swindle the dumb clucks who don't happen to live in the Hamptons and go to the same parties they do. At the very most, eighty, or maybe a hundred and some, or even a couple or three hundred crooked individuals in all. That's a tiny number when you view it in perspective. Say there's even as many as eight or ten thousand ready to clean you out, down to your parking stubs. Still, that leaves—what?—seven *billion* people on the planet? By comparison, we're talking about a very, very small number here. We heard that most of them were seasonal help and temp CEOs who weren't affiliated with us in an official capacity. And you don't have to worry, because they're basically all gone now, owing to the law of supply and demand.

It's the nature of the animal, unfortunately. In any human community, be it a used car lot or a street gang in L.A. or a

Moroccan open-air bazaar, or anywhere, you're going to have some unscrupulous people who abuse the public trust. Always have been, always will be. Investing is a crapshoot. We don't have to tell you that. You accepted those terms from the beginning. With investing, maybe you win or, then again, maybe your 401(k) shrinks down to two weeks' paid vacation before your final trip to Mass. General. We have always been up front with you. At no time did we give you reason to think this arrangement was anything other than what it is. You know the score. We always acted like grownups, you and us.

Right? Or are we wrong? Tell us. It feels like you can't confide in us anymore. There's a . . . remoteness. Okay, you need time to yourself. Regroup, lick your wounds—we can understand that. But don't take it to an extreme. That would be highly irresponsible of you. When you allow yourself to lose confidence in us, you run the risk of destroying everything. If you don't have confidence in us, force yourself to. Work hard on that particular goal. We will help you to attain it. That's what we're trying to do, with all our heart, right now.

Listen, we brought you something. G'head, open it. Ever see one of those before? That's right, it's a dividend. Try it on. Oh, that looks beautiful on you, with the chestnut brown of your portfolio. It brings out the color. You're one of the most beautiful investors in the whole world, no kidding. We know, we haven't been too attentive in the past about the little details, dividends and things, that mean a lot to an investor. We thought you understood how we felt and we didn't need to do all that. Now we see that we do. Too often we omitted those small but important displays, and we learned our lesson. We'll be better about giving you more of those from now on, we promise. Oh, and by the way—they'll all be tax-free. Already taken care of. Don't mention it. It's a change that's long overdue.

We feel funny telling you this—we don't even know if we should—but what the heck: The other day, on the street, we were talking to some associates and acquaintances whom we happened to bump into, and suddenly we said we loved you. For real. It just popped out. Everybody standing there, listening, big as life, and we don't know what came over us—we blurted out that we loved you. If you don't believe us, ask Eliot Spitzer. He was standing right there.

Do we have to get down on our knees? If that's what it takes, we will. We want you back. We're asking in all sincerity and humility. From the opening bell every morning, you're our whole world. Yes, accounting errors were made. No one disputes that. Life savings were misappropriated, regrettably. It will never, ever happen again, we swear to you. Increased anti-swindling safeguards are in place today because of the respect we have for you. You were hurt, and you had a right to be, but no amount of giving up yesterday's mansions bought with stolen money can ever restore what's gone. A wonderful future lies ahead, and we want you with us as a part of it. We need you to be there, with your boundless abundance and enthusiasm. So pick up the phone. Authorize the wire transfer. There will never be a better time to get back in than now. You know you still care for us. Please place the call. Please.

From Across the Pond

h, America! Every image of it in the films is true, I thought to myself, as my oily-featured driver sped through amber lights and babbled maniacally into his radio. The familiar smell (for this was my third visit) of a place near the airport called Queens came to my nose. Which queen, or queens, were referred to, however, no one could say. Power and greed and Machiavellian scheming filled the very air along the avenue we traveled on—Jackson Avenue, I think it was, no doubt named in honor of the famous American pop star possibly born nearby. Ferret-eyed mafiosi, underage prostitutes, neighborhood drug runners, confidence tricksters, and dreary lumpen nobodies swarmed at every crossing and roundabout. Lying back on the odoriferous upholstery, I drank in the teeming totality through every pore.

A very few of these strivers, the extraordinarily lucky and clever ones, will someday rise above their station and grab the whip hand in their country's ruthless hierarchy. Countless others will descend to the level of the mass murderer and tabloid reader in wretched rented flats, there forever to remain. I planned to steep myself in both extremes, for both are the quintessence of America. Suddenly and sharply I called out to my driver to stop the taxicab. A street-side news vendor, with an apparent nonchalance belying the untouchable lowness of his trade, approached my partly open window. I knew what the fellow wanted as well as he did—my fifty cents (American) in return for a current issue of the scandalously lurid *Daily News*. I tossed him the coins and he pocketed them, then turned in search of other prey.

Appraisingly I eyed my purchase. There on its cover—which for some reason appeared on the back of the publication rather than the front, and upside down—was a photo of the man I had crossed an ocean to meet and interview. Even from that odd position, his commanding, charismatic eyes locked with mine. A thrill of consent ran through me involuntarily; one could understand at a glance why those who knew him called George Steinbrenner "The Boss." Forget the clichés about his business acumen, forget the neo-puritan tut-tuttings over his felony conviction, and note instead the debonairness of the Steinbrenner style. A nearly feral magnetism seemed to shimmer from his surprisingly unpretentious blazer, slightly out-thrust chin, and iron-filing hair and teeth. Ruling his empire of sports teams had given him the extravagant habits of unlimited authority. His acquisitions, his tantrums, his perfectionism—all have been widely reported on, along with his enormous personal fortune, said to be the largest in much of the world.

Imagining our upcoming meeting, I had to suppress the urge to shout with excitement like a third former at a football match. (N.B.: In America, what we call football they call, for some reason, "soccer," and what they call "football" is something else entirely.) After all, this was the man famous for sack-ing an unruly employee not once but five times! How would this raw, untutored, childlike American genius respond to me? Would he dismiss me out of hand? Or would he perhaps be so taken with me and the article I plan to write that he would offer me a situation in his front office, where I would vet the many top sports players whose services he procures? And then, perhaps, I would go on to make a big splash in his organization, win the admiration of "Fran" Healy and "Joe" Torre, and secure a fabulous salary as Herr Steinbrenner's chief aide and factotum. I would own a penthouse flat on Fifth Avenue, travel on the Concorde every weekend . . .

"I'm sorry, but Mr. Steinbrenner is not available at the moment," I practiced, in my severest tones. "This is Mr. Steinbrenner's highly paid personal executive assistant. Mr. Steinbrenner cannot come to the phone because he is visiting his private holdings in Tampa, Florida. For the record, Mr. Steinbrenner has authorized me to say that some of his coaching staff did not perform up to standard during the previous postseason. He names no names. The guilty parties know they have much to answer for . . . What? I *beg* your pardon? Do you have any *idea* whom you are talking to? Who do you think you *are*?"

Overhearing this, my poor cabman cringed even lower behind the steering wheel at the forcefulness of my voice and manner.

Yes, a position with the Steinbrenner firm would be right up my street. And I would be perfect for the firm as well. Once I had stamped it with my own unmistakable watermark, Mr. S. would begin to confide in me. In the posh cabin of his private jet on our way to an invitation-only awards luncheon, I would reveal to him the outline of my grander plans. "This game your sports team plays all summer, George," I could hear myself explaining, "it's so byzantine, so of the past. The few times I've watched it on the television, I've absolutely loved it, of course. But not everybody does, I must tell you. 'Thumb-suckingly boring' is one of the kinder adjectives used. We must *do* something about that game, George.

"And while we're on the subject, George," my inner monologue continued, "may we take a look at some of the people in your employ? This fellow Zip Zimmer, for example—now, George, what exactly are this man's duties? Does anyone, including himself, even know? And what of this television and radio presenter, this Rizzuto? Is 'Scooter' really a name you want associated with any person to whom you give serious responsibility? My advice is to sack the lot of them at once, George, and begin completely anew!"

With a jolt that brought me back to earth, my taxicab stopped at the door of New York's most luxurious five-star hotel, the Q Motor Lodge, in Queens. I alighted on the pavement and retrieved my cases from the boot. My sneering, fawning driver appeared for his much-coveted fee and, once paid, sidled back into his reeking vehicle and careered off into the night. After handing my luggage to a bellman who later turned out to be merely a passerby, I received my key and ascended to my room, on the second floor. (N.B.: In America, what we call the first floor is their second, because they call what would be our ground floor their first, making their second floor one floor lower than it is for us, which nonetheless somehow does not reduce the overall height of their buildings.)

Arrived, at last! The door to my demi-suite clicked shut behind me with a subtle, moneyed sound. I strode across the room, detouring round the bed, and drew back the window curtains. There before me stretched a panorama of this vast American city in all its mystery: to my left, the wall of what appeared to be, from its many ventings, a launderette; to my right, adjacent to the wall, a car park of ten or twenty spaces, beneath a streetlamp with flickering bulb. Somewhere in that fecund, brutal, half-civilized land lay the answer to my dreams.

For a long moment I stood by the window. Then I stepped back and saw, superimposed on the view, my own face reflected in the glass. I could not help but notice how much I had changed just since Heathrow. Add one of those billed sports caps the Americans love to wear and an undershirt splashed with advertising, and I would be indistinguishable from a native. I made a mental note to buy myself both those items first thing tomorrow. Then I would go in search of the city's main outdoor arena stadium—it could not be hard to find—and proceed with my grand design. Already, however, my mind was vaulting beyond immediate achievements to others I could not even imagine, waiting invisibly offstage. As they began to take vague form, I deliberately dismissed them, in order to preserve the surprise.

Now to work. With pen and stationery provided gratis by the hotel, I sat down to record my impressions thus far.

Everlasting

The shock our family experienced at the death of our beloved uncle Simon is beyond my power to describe. You feel so helpless, so bereft . . . For months afterward we stumbled around in a fog of numbed incomprehension. But then grief naturally began to turn to anger. How could something like this have happened? Simon was a strong, healthy man of ninety-seven years. He had never been sick a single day or suffered any serious injury. In my mind, that profile sent up a red flag right away. Here's a man who has lived without any health problems at all for nearly a hundred years, and suddenly one morning, out of the blue, he dies. Obviously, the facts point to hidden negligence or other underlying causes.

A few of our acquaintances—no one close to us, of course—whispered that Simon had brought his death on himself by being "old." That blame-the-victim approach is hardly worth responding to, except to say that "old" is a relative term, and reducing anybody's life to a number seems inaccurate and unfair. One or two other people have been insensitive enough to inform us, witlessly, that "we all have to go sometime." As if such platitudes spoke to our sorrow and outrage! Yes, many human beings do "go" after a certain number of years. But do we have to? By no means. In Simon's case, there wasn't a reason in the world for this man to die. Simon's blood pressure was at exactly the level posted on the AMA's website, and when they lowered the recommendation not long ago, Simon's pressure, amazingly, went down just enough to meet it. His heartbeat, circulation, kidney and liver function, lungs, motility—all the indicators were right where they should be for a perfectly functioning metabolism.

And when it came to the life-enhancing qualities of attitude and involvement, Uncle Simon was simply off the charts. He was the sweetest, kindest, most thoughtful, generous, wonderful man. Anyplace he went, he lit it up with his spirit. If you saw the pleasure he took just from his clay class . . . What possible purpose could have been served by the death of such a man? Now we understand, in human terms, what it means to be a throwaway society.

Uncle Simon used to tell the most marvelous stories. He was in the merchant marine and his family owned one of the first television sets in Canton, Ohio. We would listen to him by the hour, but unfortunately none of us ever thought to sit down with him in front of a tape recorder and preserve his stories for the future. Now we never will. What's especially hard about his death is that it's so final.

Simon's children, who were more involved than anyone else in his health maintenance, feel that modern science is to blame. They believe that it largely ignores people in Simon's situation and, instead of helping, hides behind statistics and actuarial tables. These, however, when examined more closely, reveal a picture that is strikingly different from what we've all been told. It's true that most people in our country die in their seventies and eighties. Surprisingly, though, far fewer of them die in their early hundreds; or, to put it another way, people who approach that more advanced age are actually *less* likely to die. These hardy folks have survived the most perilous of life's passages, and are stronger for it, and usually are geared up and ready to live on and on. An enlightened science responsive to their needs would provide them with the appropriate medicines and technological tools, instead of devoting most of its resources to fields like cosmetic-surgery research, which it does because (quite frankly) that's where the money is.

Behind this administrative failing is an even bigger one—a failing of human imagination. Nowhere is it engraved in stone that a person's life must last for only so long. The Bible's dreary statement that a life span is "three-score years and ten" and its tired talk about times to be born and times to die now smell strongly of plain old defeatism. Determined individuals like Noah and Mickey Rooney have shown that people can live indefinitely beyond what is thought of as normal chronology. The members of the rock group Aerosmith, by suspending their pulse rates and similar techniques, have managed to survive and remain a touring band since the days of the French and Indian War. They provide a goal that the rest of us can work toward.

In simplest terms, it's only common sense: if we're still living, why stop? And yet for centuries we've accepted the myth of life as a "natural" cycle, with a beginning, a middle, and an end, conveniently overlooking our own responsibility in it. Were Uncle Simon here, I'm sure he would agree. He did all that could be expected in order to remain on the planet, but a shortsighted, too-little-too-late public policy on this subject sadly let him down.

For my part, I plan to keep on looking into larger systemic problems that could have contributed somehow to my uncle's death. Even more, I intend to make sure that what happened to him doesn't happen to me. Preparation will be the key, so I've begun by taking a personal health inventory. I am sixty-three years old, not that it matters, and I could lose sixty or eighty pounds, though I'm comfortable at my present weight. Other than that, I'm in excellent shape. I do have a mild case of gynecomastia, some anal seepage, and hip, knee, and bladder problems, with substantial loss of hearing, sight, and sense of smell. Those aside, I'm just the same, physically, as I was at twenty-five.

And mentally I'm even younger. I refuse to be categorized as "senior" in what I think or do. I keep up with popular culture and pay attention to (and wear) the latest young-adult styles. I never miss a new movie aimed at the youth market, and though adult critics may decry such movies, I enjoy them, and admire their vitality. I'm careful to maintain a youthful outlook even in the language I use; for example, I avoid the word "aging," because of its negative connotation. I prefer to think that as years go by a person isn't aging but continuing. I plan to continue for a very long time.

In an absolute worst-case scenario, forty years from now I and all the rest of us sixty-somethings will be gone. This dire prediction for the future is of course only one of many, and may or may not come to pass. It should make us stop and think, however. If it did happen, it would represent a serious disruption in the way we live now. To understand it better, imagine the sun coming up exactly as it did this morning; the year, however, is 2043, and you are not there, anywhere on earth, to see it, and neither is anyone you went to school with, knew from work, or used to run into around town. The prospect is deeply unsettling, and should motivate everybody to action. Those at risk should start making phone calls, firing off e-mails, and contacting congressional representatives. The oncoming threat can be averted with proper use of technology and sufficient funding, but efforts must begin soon if they are to succeed. As we've learned, to our sorrow, not enough will be done unless we push as hard as we can.

Class Notes

J ack **"Spicer" Conant** tells us that when he was in Houston recently on a business trip, he put in a call to Houstonite and classmate **Chuck Gales**, but Chuck didn't call back.

Jim Carmichael writes that he happened to see **Marc Weinstein** in the Salt Lake City airport not long ago and pretended not to recognize him.

Out of the blue the other day, **Bill Tolan** says, he realized he had forgotten the names of **Marty Glimer**, **Todd Saalsten**, and **Andy Camp**. A quick glance at our yearbook refreshed his memory.

Ann (Patterson) Simms asks, "What in the world was I thinking of, going out with **Mike Stack**?" Don't know, Annie—but are you sure his name wasn't **Russ**?

Arthur Stancik never liked **Jim McMickens**, and hasn't seen him in years.

From rainy Seattle, **Alex Kostygian** sends a note inquiring about "the name of the **skinny black guy** who was in our class for a few weeks at the beginning of sophomore year and then dropped out." Sorry we can't help you with that, Alex!

Fuadh Akmed Muhammad says he now can't believe he ever went to school here.

Though **Geoff Emery** sat next to **Hotch Engleman** at every assembly for four years, today he can't bring his face to mind.

Mariah Miller told **Judith (Mandelbaum) Giles** and **Lacie (Stone) McCarthy** she'd love to have lunch, but doesn't get into the city that often. Judith, or maybe Lacie, had just returned from Italy.

Benjamin Kaplan, recently downsized, wonders why he should donate money to a school he can't afford to send his own children to. Ben, you've got us there!

When **Marylin Cho** saw **Tony Lemire**'s name on her caller ID last summer, she let the machine pick up. Her daughter, **Sophie** ('06), later erased the message by mistake.

Gus Trebonyek and **Ted Antrim**, who lived just one floor apart in Brainard junior and senior years, never met once during that entire time. Gus went on to a career in law, and Ted eventually became a consultant with a management firm. Ted moved to far-off Anchorage, Alaska. Gus, meanwhile, settled into a successful practice as a litigator in Detroit. Finally, as middle-aged men with wives and families, both Ted and Gus came back for the twenty-fifth reunion, where again their paths did not cross. They still don't know each other from Adam.

A luncheon buffet and cash bar at the Westin Hotel gave class members in the San Francisco area a chance for catching up and reminiscing last month. **Spencer Beale**, who attended, reports that nobody there looked at all familiar, and he thinks he might have been in the wrong room.

Wasn't **Kay Fortunaro** a number, with those tight sweaters she used to wear? Well, turns out that was someone else. A misidentification of a photo in our Class Register is to blame.

The secretary of **Fisk Pettibone** passes along the welcome news that "of course he remembers [us]" and will drop us a note when he has time.

MOVIN' ON: Often, mail sent to classmates returns unopened, but with a little sleuthing we discovered that **Melanie Ostroff** hasn't lived at the address we have for her since 1985! The house, a two-bedroom Colonial, belonged to her parents, who bought it in the 1960s and have since died. The current residents went to public schools.

Mitchell DiMario, **Sallie Stark**, **Chris Feinstock**, **Joel Bushwell**, and **Will "Thirsty" Tabor** all rented cars for business travel on weekends within the past year, thus qualifying for certain perks and discounts. They may meet to talk about this next fall.

Bruce Dunlop couldn't pick **Tim Brandt**, **Roger Magnuson**, or **Larry Bollardi** out of a police lineup today. He hasn't a clue what became of them, or whether he might have confused them with some guys he used to hang out with at a summer camp in Maine.

Guy Forstman says he left **Rick Kelling**'s business card in the pocket of a suit that's at the cleaners, or possibly in a drawer at the office. Guy is sure it will turn up.

On the way to a sales appointment recently, **Bob Halmer** drove right by the campus. Though going fairly fast, he appeared to look much the same.

Cecily Spaeth-McCorkle makes more than any of her

former teachers, according to a newsy e-mail she sent from the south of France.

Married the week after graduation, classmates **Alison Stammel** and **Randy Tinsley** divorced acrimoniously long ago. Both report that they are better off.

Wilson Yoshida very rarely thinks about anything having to do with his past, and throws away all letters or circulars bearing the school's return address. Wilson was the 2002 recipient of a "no-limits" checking account.

Lyle Kerner simply disappeared.

McMurdo Station, a lonely research outpost in Antarctica near the South Pole, has to be the last place on earth where you'd expect to run into your roommate from sophomore year. If anyone ever does, please write or call with details.

We have received the following from **Katie (Cole) Shearwood**, firing off a missive in the midst of her busy schedule: "Hello, all! As we formerly youthful (don't remind me!) friends and classmates wend our way closer to codger-hood, I can't help but sit back and wonder. What I'll be when I grow up is still up for grabs, though perhaps less so now than ever before. In '99 I left my longtime job as a group vice president responsible for more than eight hundred people in a pre-public biotech company dealing with infrastructure issues—enjoyed the work, but felt a change was due—and founded KatieCorp, my own firm handling on-demand biosecurity auditing and database vulnerability analysis. Who would've guessed? I absolutely love it, and only regret that I didn't make the change weeks earlier. Plus, as an added bonus, I met my current spouse/partner/best friend/severest critic/terrific lover, Dennie Strube. (Dennie Shearwood, my ex, is history, though we remain good friends, and I kept his name.) I quickly had three children to add to my previous two and his four, and before we knew it all had left for colleges and graduate schools, where they are doing splendidly. I remain very concerned about the state of our nation and the world. As a new empty nester, I find I have more time to think about what I, as a generation, have accomplished for right (and wrong). The success of KatieCorp, whose factories are now in Suriname and run themselves, causes me to look for new challenges. When I see my face in the mirror in the morning, peering between the lines for the hopeful young person I once was, I say, 'Katie—,' and then I tell myself various things. I've had to juggle so much (I'm with a small local circus here in Montreal), and yet I still get up every morning eager for what the day will bring, and no man I'd care to drink with would do otherwise."

Does anybody have any idea who Katie was?

Back in the U.S.A.

The Pentagon is drawing up a new kind of bird. Code-named Project Falcon, the new "hypersonic cruise vehicle" would fly at more than 5,000 mph and drop bombs anywhere in the world in just two hours. The aircraft would allow the U.S. to launch bombing raids from U.S. soil and avoid reliance on overseas bases—and the approval of touchy foreign governments . . . The aircraft—which has a target date of 2025—would carry 12,000 pounds of smart bombs, special forces operators or smaller unmanned drones.

—*Daily News*, August 4, 2003

Pam Cerilla pushed open her kitchen door, set two bulging bags of groceries on the counter, and picked up the quickly scrawled note her husband had left for her: "Pam—Had to go back to the base. Don't wait supper. Bombing Iceland. Love you, Randy." With a resigned sigh, she began putting the frozen food away. Knowing Randy, he had probably been so jazzed at getting back to that big bird of his that he'd forgotten the little details—like finding someone to fill in for him at hockey practice. Oh, well, she could substitute-coach tonight. Lord knows she'd done it before.

Driving to pick up their middle son at swimming lessons, she allowed herself an undutiful moment of impatience. What was the problem with those Icelanders, anyway? Why couldn't they get the hang of American-style democracy? The United States had moved into that country over a year ago, when our president began to worry that the prime minister of Iceland "had looked at him funny" during a meeting between the two. The regime change had been over fast, and then there were supposed to be just a few "touch-up" bombings to get the process to democratic rule on track. But here they'd called Randy three times already this month to re-bomb some targets they said had not been bombed in a democracy-inducing way the first time. Occasionally they'd call him to go bomb something at three in the morning. Didn't they know he had family responsibilities, too?

At least Iceland was a quick turnaround. He'd be back tonight early enough that he could get up in the morning with the kids and let her sleep in. Randy was better than most of the hypersonic-cruise-vehicle pilots at sharing child-care duties. When they weren't flying five thousand miles an hour, the other guys in Randy's wing usually just lay around playing video games and reading Locke and Hume. They were an elite unit, equally schooled in the latest weapons systems and democratic theory, and proud to the point of cockiness. From bitter comments she'd heard other wives make, she knew that most of their husbands rarely lifted a finger around the house.

She should be grateful for her nice home and happy children and helpful spouse, really she should—and yet just at the moment she didn't have it in her. Once admitted, doubts and complaints began crowding her mind. For example, why didn't they ever schedule missions in a way that fit a family's schedule? She couldn't count the number of birthday parties and family outings she'd carefully arranged, only to have the phone ring, and then off he'd go. Back when America was revamping the whole Denmark-Norway-Sweden area—a year and a half ago? two years?—had been the worst. The long flights, odd hours, and complicated drops were a nightmare for Randy. Keeping all those cities straight, with who got what—cruise missiles for Oslo, special forces operators for Trondheim, wire-guided voting booths for Stockholm—gave him fits. He would come home and collapse into bed, too tired to watch his mission's results on the evening news.

Fortunately, Denmark (and Norway and Sweden) had been swiftly defeated. We had renamed the entire area "Vikingland," in a culturally sensitive gesture to its past, and then the hard work of democracy building had begun. The tech wizards fitted Randy's plane with rockets, or maybe rays—the details were classified, so Pam didn't know for sure—specially designed to cause New England–style town meetings to spring up within a thousand meters of impact. That did the trick, and soon the place was better than it had ever been before, and a model of America's success at modernizing out-of-date governments. But then we'd inherited the whole Faroe Islands problem, which entangled us with Iceland . . .

How many countries *were* there in the world anyway? Pam's head swam trying to imagine them all. It seemed the minute we'd get a country fixed up and running, another one halfway around the globe would go on the blink. People did not appreciate how hard dedicated airmen like Randy had to work, jetting here to straighten out one mess, then there to handle the next. Half of the places the press didn't even bother to report on anymore. Like the morning Randy bombed the Dominican Republic and the island of Dominica, in order to get them to make their names less confusing. That had been Randy's idea, done on his own initiative, and he could've been disciplined for it. But it got no coverage, and when the president heard about it through the international grapevine, he just said it seemed like a good idea to him, and there the matter ended.

According to the scuttlebutt in the flight briefing room, Randy said, the next big project was New Zealand. The objective would be to test a new policy of pre-pre-preemption, or pre-$_3$-emption, by which countries were attacked more preemptively than usual "to fake everybody out," as Randy explained. Frankly, she didn't understand the strategic thinking behind a lot of Randy's assignments, and she didn't try to. She'd known what she was signing on for when she married him. Her job was to provide support and encouragement and not ask questions about certain topics. It was a deal she could live with, all in all. At least he wasn't stationed far away in some touchy, unreliable foreign country.

Errands accomplished, Pam pulled into her driveway and let the engine idle awhile, so the kids could keep watching their video in the backseat. Turning the air-conditioning up a notch, she leaned back and enjoyed the feeling of secure comfort in her vehicle, a civilian version of an armored personnel carrier. Randy had bought it for them, he said, because he wanted them to be extra, extra safe. She rolled down the window and listened for a second to catch the extremely loud sound of her husband's hypersonic plane roaring across the sky, but all she heard was the rumbling of other planes and cars, including her own.

She longed for the day when pilots would fly their planes by remote control from computers on the ground. Then maybe Randy would be able to do most of his work from home. For the present, they had to make the best of the technology that existed, labor-intensive and inconvenient though it might be. Countries everywhere depended on us to make them more like America and to redirect them when they began to go wrong. Deep down, Pam felt this responsibility almost personally. Right now, she knew, Randy was on his way back, pedal to the metal, the smoking skyline of Reykjavík or wherever disappearing behind. Probably he was wondering if his favorite meal would be keeping warm in the oven when he returned. In a couple of hours, she thought, he would walk through the back door having done his job. With a renewed sense of purpose, she set about to do hers.

He, the Murderer

The murderer can't find a parking space. A hard morning spent murdering people, and now this. He has errands to run, the murderer. What a week he's had, and it's only Thursday. Just look at his schedule:

Monday   murder somebody

Tuesday   murder somebody

Wednesday   sit around

Thursday   murder somebody; do errands

The average person has no idea what a murderer goes through, the murderer thinks, shaking his head ruefully. All you ever hear about are the victims. Being a murder victim is tough, no question about that. But, afterward, who gets stuck with the cleanup? This particular murderer is a complicated person, not an animal like some murderers. He drives to Costco to buy shower-curtain rings on a Thursday afternoon, same as anybody. And now some jerk has taken up two spaces, when the parking lot is completely full! The murderer thinks people who do that should be murdered.

To himself, he doesn't use the word "murdered." He uses the word "whacked," or, sometimes, "taken out." Hey, he's not an English professor—he's a murderer. Actually, for a while when he was younger, he wanted to be an English professor. Enrolled in college courses and everything. He got a lot out of it—*The Faerie Queene*. Weird to think he ever read a book with a title like that. The life wasn't right for him, though. On an aptitude test, "Murderer" was the category he scored highest in. By then, he'd already murdered a couple of guys, just fooling around. He kind of liked it. One thing led to another.

Now he wishes he'd murdered more people when he was younger. You reach the age of forty, forty-five, and you can't react like you used to when you were twenty. Just starting out as a young murderer, he was amazing, with a new move every time. He'd be talking to one person, threatening to murder him, and then all of a sudden he'd reach around and shoot the guy standing next to him right in the head. Nobody'd ever done that before. He'd shoot guys over his shoulder or through his legs, shoot them while he was on the telephone ordering the contract murders of other guys. He was doing what everybody secretly would love to do if they weren't too scared, and it gave him an adrenaline rush. And then somewhere along the way it started to become a chore.

Everybody's got his hand out these days, wanting a favor. "Hey, Ronnie, can you murder my nephew?" "Ronnie, my man, if you got a second, could you murder the head of the Plumbers and Contractors Union?" "Yo, Uncle Ronnie, how about doing a little murdering for us, pro bono?" Like always, friends and family take advantage. The murderer tries to help out when he can. He's an obliging guy. He also has a surprisingly strong set of family values. Been married for twenty-two years to the same woman—Felicity, a skilled murderess. In her day, she won some real street cred, the murderer fondly recalls. Now she's retired, or semiretired. She was something: used to confuse people with gymnastics, and then—*chop!*—cut them almost in half with a big sword. She's put on weight since then, so now she uses fertilizer bombs. When she still murders people, that is, which is seldom.

The murderer and his wife have a son whom he adores. The murderer's face softens and gets very tender when he thinks about him. Always calls him "my boy." To hear him talk about that son of his would break your heart, if he weren't murdering you. He is determined that his son will not have to murder people when he gets big, and will be able to make a good living simply by injuring them. Right now, that is his dream. Sometimes he'll come home in the evening, blood still under his fingernails, and sit down at the dining-room table with his son to help him build a model plane or finish a spelling assignment. No human being is easy to explain. The murderer doesn't pretend to be.

At this point, some errors should be cleared up. When the murderer earlier allowed the inference that he planned to shop at Costco, he misspoke. In fact, he never intended to shop there, and he considers it a place for idiots and mooks. Instead, he planned to shop at a home-furnishings store that he prefers not to be too specific about. Okay, it was Home Depot. So now the murderer goes into Home Depot, finds the items he came for, buys them, goes back to the parking lot, murders somebody (the guy who took up two spaces—serves him right), and leaves the guy laying on the asphalt. (Note to grammarians, re the "lie-lay" solecism: *Give up*, already! You've lost!) The dead guy is laying there all shot up, one eye hanging from the socket like some goofy Halloween mask, plasma already separating out of the pool of blood beside him, flies buzzing around. Murderer gets in his car and drives off.

It's funny the things you remember. This thought crosses the murderer's mind as he maneuvers his car along the familiar streets of his suburban neighborhood.

Yes, it's funny the things you remember.

Now the murderer hears the sound of a helicopter right overhead. This problem again! The murderer begins to drive fast and run over pedestrians and fruit stands. Coincidentally, a number of other murderers in the vicinity at that time are also trying to get away from law-enforcement agencies who are after them. Some of the murderers are running from the FBI, some from the CIA, some from Alcohol, Tobacco, and Firearms, and a few just from the local police. Many of the streets the murderer usually takes when pursued are closed due to police actions. While backing up from a roadblock and making a turn on two wheels, the murderer crashes into two other murderers. He gets out of his car and murders them, saving the state the trouble. Then he walks over to several U.S. marshals who have screeched to a stop nearby and he patiently explains the circumstances and who he is. Impressed, they loan him one of their unmarked cars so he can go home.

A couple of blocks away, the murderer has second thoughts

and goes back and murders the marshals also. No point in taking chances, and anyway, why not? Today is a special day. Today the murderer's son turns nine years old. The murderer and his wife have been planning the party for months. He passes a novelty store and stops in to buy some paper hats. At the cash register, he flirts with the salesgirl, and she responds warmly. The truth is, aside from the killing, the murderer has a basically good heart. People sense that about him, and if they survive they are drawn to him. Deep, deep under that blood-and-tissue-spattered exterior is a giving and generous man.

Who are you to judge him, anyhow? You have probably committed a few murders yourself, though you won't acknowledge it. Think back. When you put rat poison in the food of a business rival, and he later ate the food and died, you share in the responsibility, however indirectly, for his death. Each one of us has similar uncomfortable episodes in our past. The very fact that we are still walking the planet is a good indication that at some previous moment we deliberately caused someone's death to benefit our own lives. So it's better not to look too closely beneath the veil. That is why we need the murderer. He is us, minus our false fronts, shame, and "law-abiding" behavior. In fact, let's be even more honest than we were being before. We not only resemble the murderer, and need the murderer, we like and admire the murderer and think he's so great that we would want him for a friend. We hope he keeps murdering, at his own discretion, as many murder victims as he wants, except for our own family and friends (or most of them). A lifetime of murdering has given the murderer a wisdom and a higher consciousness that the rest of timid humanity will never understand. He's a murderer, okay? Let him be.

No. Please, No

It happened a few months ago. I wanted to tell you about it at the time, but somehow I couldn't. I guess I needed to process it myself. I still haven't completely come to terms with it, but at least now I can talk about it. I know I was not straightforward with you, and I should have been. Forgive me.

This isn't going to be easy. There's no good way to say it, so:

Tom Ford has left Gucci.

I'm sorry. I know what hearing this does to you. He has left Gucci, Domenico has left with him, they're both gone, end of story.

It sounds so stark, a sentence that should never be said: *Tom Ford has left Gucci*. But it's all too true. Yes, I've had the same thoughts, over and over, that you're having now. Yes, the fact that his contract was not renewed is senseless and baffling and self-destructive of Gucci as a company. I wish I had more comfort to give. Sometimes things happen that we simply can't explain.

There's no rhyme or reason—I don't want to think about it, and yet somehow I can't stop. No designer knows luxury better than Tom Ford; Gucci is the most important luxury-products company in the world; and so Gucci management decides . . . to let Tom Ford *go*? Am I missing something here?

The fact remains that Tom Ford has left Gucci. I keep going over it. I can't help myself. It's like I'm numb. Tom. Ford. Has left. Gucci. I mean, everyone knew Tom Ford was *thinking* of leaving Gucci. That rumor had been around for months, or even years. But thinking of leaving and actually leaving are two different things. As the models walked down the runway at his last show, in Paris, the finality of it sank in with the spectators: "This is it. He's really leaving. Tom Ford is actually leaving Gucci." People began to sob. André Leon Talley, a giant of a man, sat there with his shoulders just heaving. It had come to this.

An instant later, people were rushing for the exits. Nobody had been able to believe it, and now that it was happening they needed to tell the community at large. A luxury-goods analyst who won't let me use her name, due to grief, had her staff stencil "Tom Ford Is Leaving Gucci" on the front of her limo, specifying that it be reversed and backward— "iɔɔuƆ ǫniʌɒɘ⅃ ꙅI bɿoꟻ moT"—so that drivers in cars up ahead could read it and yield the road. Hazard lights flashing, she roared away into the Parisian night.

As for me, I only wanted to go off somewhere by myself and curl into a ball. Instead, I ended up having a quiet dinner with friends, and we talked of other matters, trying to lift one another's spirits and pretending all the while that we weren't failing miserably.

Over time, we would learn that there are seven stages a person goes through when Tom Ford leaves Gucci. The first is shock and rage. The second is also shock and rage, with rage starting to predominate. The third is pretty much all rage; I forget the stages after that, because I'm still partly in shock. During the rage period, it is quite natural to put a lot of blame on Serge Weinberg, the CEO of the faceless, soulless company that owns Gucci, who indeed has much to answer for. Obviously, Serge Weinberg must be a very disturbed person to have done such a thing. But simply blaming Serge Weinberg and letting it go at that overlooks deeper and more systemic problems.

Serge Weinberg does not truly understand luxury. Tom Ford has said as much, and no one disputes that he is correct. But what does "luxury" mean? I think all of us in the luxury-products milieu know better than to try to pin it down. Putting it another way, "luxury" is a mystical awareness of luxury that a very few extraordinary individuals simply *have*. The full meaning can't be contained in a single word, which is why many initiates prefer to spell it "l*x*r*." In a practical sense, however, "luxury" may be described as the calling, or vocation, to make newer and more luxurious luxury products than the ones that have previously been made. This is what Tom Ford, above all others, has repeatedly proved he can do.

But how to convey that persuasively to someone like Serge Weinberg? (And I'm not singling him out here; okay, I am, but he's a part of the larger non-luxury-sensitive corporate culture.) How to get through to the kinds of people who can't comprehend, and never will, what makes a luxury pair of sunglasses "luxury"? Or, as another example, consider this particular Gucci handbag. It is not a luxury handbag because it is hand-sewn from chic black leather with pink stripes or because it also includes a satin web and detachable shoulder chain. No—

what makes it a real luxury handbag is the full-size enameled brass horse bit extending luxuriously across it from one end to the other. Would Serge Weinberg or the rest of the higher-ups at his company have thought in a million years to add that enameled brass horse bit? One need say no more.

Strangely enough, I'm starting to feel better now. Confronting the sentence "Tom Ford has left Gucci," as I'm doing here, deprives it of some of its primal power to terrify. I repeat it out loud, in my normal voice, calmly: "Tom Ford has left Gucci." And you see? The words are spoken, yet the earth continues to turn, the sun still shines, the flowers—

Oh, hell! Who am I kidding? I try to put on a brave face, and then it goes all to smash! *Why was this leaving allowed to occur?* Why did nobody stop that crazed fiend Serge Weinberg? Why didn't some courageous person at Pinault-Printemps-Redoute (Serge Weinberg's company) come to his or her senses and alter the fateful course before it was too late? And what about the rest of us? Why did *we* just sit idly by? Tom Ford left, irrevocably, and Domenico with him, and the rest of us did, for all intents and purposes, NOTHING. Tom Ford says he's going to Hollywood to become a filmmaker, which is great, but again I ask the painful question: Why? What greater purpose is served by a man who understands luxury going into movies, a medium in which, frankly, any reasonably talented designer can succeed? I know I should accept what can't be changed, but I am not able to, and I refuse to. "Tom Ford has left Gucci." Make it not true.

If Memory Doesn't Serve

Among the cruelest tricks life plays is the way it puts the complicated part at the end, when the brain is declining into simplicity, and the simple part at the beginning, when the brain is fresh and has memory power to spare. As a boy I had only a few things to keep track of. There was one place, the small town where I lived; two pro sports, baseball and football; three TV channels; four sequential seasons, as yet unmixed by global warming; five kids in my neighborhood to play with; and so on. In no category did the number of entries go much above a dozen or two. I didn't meet people and have to remember their names, because everybody I ran into I already knew. With my extra, leftover memory I preserved pointless conversations, nonsense phrases my brother made up, remarks by adults they later claimed they hadn't said, and incidental data such as the farthest point up our street from which it was possible to run and still catch the school bus.

Since then, my memory has been required to hold gigantically much more, the bulk of it so dull. Feats of adult remembering often conform to the "negative Disneyland" rule of grown-up pleasures: that is, it is fun, of a sort, suddenly to remember where you left the registration stickers for your car, but only in comparison to the trip to the Department of Motor Vehicles you would have to make if you didn't. I sometimes nearly crumble in self-pity at the mnemonic brain-busters life hands me. An example: A few years ago the friends my young son usually played with were Joshua, Rhys, and Julian. No memory problems there—each interesting and lively boy easily matched with his name in my mind. The mothers of the boys, however, were (respectively) Georgeanne, Geraldine, and Gabrielle. To a person whose days of high-detail remembering are gone, those are essentially the same name. When greeting someone, it is not enough to know that her name begins with a G. I held this unfair complicatedness against each of them and acted put-upon and odd around them.

Does anyone remember the name of Russ Nixon, catcher for the Cleveland Indians in 1958? Once I spent lonely hours trying to remember it, and when morning came and I could call a friend who knew, I understood what had happened. My friend spoke and the name emerged, good as new, from the later Nixon overlays that had hidden it. The brain has only so many slots, and by the time you reach fifty, they have become cluttered and full. I'm sure most of us have a small place in our brains containing the following four items:

1. H. G. Wells
2. George Orwell
3. Orson Welles
4. Orson Bean

They cluster together through some unknown law of the synapses. The first two are easy to confuse because both are

1930s-era, English, and science-fictiony (*The Time Machine*, *Nineteen Eighty-four*). The second and third blend because George Orwell and Orson Welles, as names, sound like made-up, roman-à-clef versions of each other. Also, Welles did a famous hoax radio broadcast of Wells's *War of the Worlds*, a confusing event in itself. And then you have Orson Bean, who is in there probably just to round out the conjugation, or through one of those comic mishaps he used to get into in his roles as an actor. Sometimes when I have a spare moment, I take each name out, consider it, link it to the proper person, recall each one's face and biography, and then put all the names back in place in my mind. I believe this is a basically healthy exercise, like flossing.

Then, if I'm feeling like it, or if I'm still lying awake, I run through a few more calisthenics to keep myself sharp. AA is not the same as Triple A—a fact I learn and relearn at car-rental counters when I ask for an AA discount. Michael Moore, the activist author and documentary filmmaker, once made a movie called *Roger and Me*, partly about Roger Smith, then the president of General Motors. Consequently, it is quite natural to slip up and refer to Michael Moore as Roger Moore. The two are different, however; Roger Moore is a suave-seeming English movie actor who used to play James Bond, a couple of James Bonds ago. And speaking of that, I am me, and not James Bond's creator, Ian Fleming, the late English intelligence officer and author of spy thrillers. Twice now while I've been on book tours the person introducing me to the audience at a reading has said, "And now, please join me in welcoming Ian Fleming." After the second time I took to carrying a copy of *Goldfinger*, just to be ready, but so far it hasn't happened again.

Jamie Bassett was my son's third-grade teacher; Diana Tackett was my daughter's second-grade teacher. Kathy York was my daughter's third-grade teacher, Drury Thorp was my son's second-grade teacher. (Drury Thorp is related to the humorist Robert Benchley, who still has his own slot in my mind.) Ashanti is not the same as Beyoncé; the former is a popular singer who recently appeared on the cover of a New York newspaper carrying a handbag printed with a greatly enlarged photograph of her own face; the latter is a popular singer who has won several Grammy Awards and who performed the national anthem at the Super Bowl—the Janet Jackson one. Russell Means and Dennis Banks were both leaders of the American Indian Movement back in the 1970s; I am prone to refer to either or both as Russell Banks, who is neither, but a well-known novelist. Victor Klemperer, the German writer, kept a detailed two-volume journal of his days in Berlin during World War II, and has been called "the great diarist of the Holocaust"; Werner Klemperer is the American television and movie actor who played Colonel Klink on the TV series *Hogan's Heroes.* (Remarkably, Werner and Victor were cousins.)

Suddenly a nagging thought occurs to me: There is Ashanti, and there is Beyoncé . . . but wasn't there a third in that category? Yes. There was another like them—another young, model-beautiful black woman singer usually referred to by a single name. She has recently disappeared over the music-scene horizon. Her big hit song was "The Boy Is Mine." She sang it as a duet with somebody. I saw the video of it many times. In it she did a lot of voguing, hand gestures, framing her face with her fingers, and so forth. I used to do a lip-synch imitation of her, using the same gestures but ending with one of my own, which was to lift my baseball cap above my head twice with both hands. I showed my imitation often to my teenage daughter and her friends, embarrassing her. What was that singer's name? It was . . . Brandy! Thank you, memory. Ashanti, Beyoncé, and Brandy.

Jamie Bassett, Diana Tackett; Drury Thorp, Kathy York. The names of elementary school teachers have a strange power to evoke the past. Ashanti, Beyoncé, Brandy. I am slightly afraid there's yet another in that category I've forgotten about, but I won't worry over it now. Russell Means (AIM), Russell Banks (novelist), Dennis Banks (AIM). Victor Klemperer, diarist of the Holocaust; Werner Klemperer, actor who played Colonel Klink. When I have all the names straight, maybe I will get to sleep.

F. Scott Fitzgerald, whom I confuse with nobody, once said that the measure of a first-rate intellect is its ability to hold two contradictory ideas at the same time. I believe this may be one of those profound sayings that fall apart if you examine them closely. Holding two contradictory ideas simultaneously is a stunt that millions of minds pull off every day. A fifth of the people on the planet believe that their spouse is both the most wonderful person alive and the biggest disaster that ever happened to them; many of the inhabitants, sophisticated or not, of New York and Los Angeles will affirm in a single conversation that theirs is both the best and the worst city in the world. In fact, holding contradictory ideas simultaneously is a snap, because they are so distinct, and thus unlikely to interpenetrate dizzyingly with each other and swap themselves around.

A better gauge of mental subtlety, it seems to me, is whether you can retain ideas that are very similar but also different. For example, can you simultaneously think of, while noting the differences between, the dancer-actresses Rita Moreno and Chita Rivera? If you can accomplish that, try upping the ante by adding the actresses Carmen Miranda and Ida Lupino. Now see if you can hold all four in your mind simultaneously. The world of TV and movies offers many such tests. It takes all my mind's agility to hold at once the actresses Sarah Jessica Parker and Jennifer Aniston. The first step is not to think about Sarah Michelle Gellar or Sally Jessy Raphael, because that will only confuse things. Sarah Jessica Parker and Jennifer Aniston are both young, blond, beautiful, and wise-cracking but vulnerable. Both were in successful TV series that just ended. The first is married to Matthew Broderick, the second used to be married to Brad Pitt. Sarah has wavy hair; Jennifer's is straight. Thinking of one somehow makes it almost impossible to think of the other. Both are in the news a lot, which allows more chances to practice.

Then there are Charles Durning and Brian Dennehy (Wilford Brimley being the confusing third in that category); Fernando Lamas and Ricardo Montalban (José Ferrer, ditto); Norman Fell and Jack Klugman; Van Heflin and Red Buttons; Swoosie Kurtz and Stockard Channing; Wally Cox and Don Knotts . . . My only advice about untangling the whole Lee Majors/William Shatner/Chad Everett/Robert Wagner/Robert Conrad/William Conrad nexus is: Don't go there. As actors from old TV series recede in time, memory conflates them into a single ur–TV star. Recently I've found that even the movie stars Robert De Niro and Al Pacino are starting to blur together in my mind.

The other day, while cleaning the house, I pointed to the dustpan in the corner of the living room and asked my daughter, "Could you please bring me the spatula?" She asked, "You mean the dustpan?" I replied—taking a page from her book—"Whatever." A dustpan and a spatula really are a lot alike. Why use a separate word for each object? "Dustpan" is drab and colorless, whereas "spatula" is a poetic-sounding creation that just rolls off the tongue. Also, "spatula" has a venerable history as a comic key word, like "rutabaga" and "Buick" and "schnauzer." So why not call both objects "spatula"? That's the decision I've made. "Spatula" might not be quite accurate when applied to a dustpan, but for most practical purposes it's close enough. As you get older, you don't want to waste time on tiny details.

On the other hand, you don't want to become so carried away with "spatula" that you repeat it over and over to yourself as you lie in bed late at night. It's a perfect example of the kind of word that, if repeated often enough, will make you insane.

If despair is a sin (and it is—it's an aspect of the deadly sin of sloth), the virtuous person must resist it, and all tendencies likely to lead to it. Torturing the mind with minutiae is one of those. Originally, I seem to recall, America took pride in its plainspoken rejection of all the pomp and foofaraw of corrupt, overcomplicated Europe. Now America is complication itself. Look down the table at the public library where people plug in their laptops, and see the heaped-up entanglements of cables and wires. Try to read the pamphlet in six-point type that your new phone carrier sends you when you change long-distance service. Go to the supermarket to buy an ordinary item for your spouse. The other day at the A&P I noticed a man lost in thought in front of a bank of different kinds of brownie mix. Then he took out his cell phone and made a call: "Hi, babe . . . You wanted Triple Chunk? Okay . . . I thought you said Triple *Fudge* Chunk." At some point the brain, in order to avoid despair, begins to shut down.

My son, who is eleven, has a memory like wet cement. Occurrences leave impressions on it and are there to stay—clear, manifest, close at hand. Like apparently all children today, he has an effortless affinity with gadgetry that exhausts me just to look at it. I call him when I want some advanced appliance turned off or on. Even more useful is his ability to replay data he has observed. Ask him what we were talking about before we started talking about what we're talking about now, and he knows. He always retrieves the thread of a conversation in a manner that's matter-of-fact or bored.

For me, however, the feeling at these moments is a vast and happy relief. When you've been trying to remember something and you suddenly remember it, the mental pleasure is keen. Not remembering eats at you, but remembering soothes and re-soothes. I imagine that feeling might be what heaven is like. You pop through to the other side, and suddenly every question you have wondered about for years and then given up on is answered. The fate of an object lost in childhood, the names of people met only once at a cocktail party, the difference between William Conrad and Robert Conrad—every answer coming to you in a limpid rush of enlightenment, as if you'd known it all along.

Kid Court

1. Elephant or No?

During sleepover, preschoolers A and Z were in A's room for "talking," a quiet time intended for winding down prior to bed. Conversation turned to recently rented cartoon movie, *Dumbo*. A remarked that "Dumbo is a cute little elephant." In response, Z stated, flatly, "Dumbo is not an elephant." Shocked by this, A replied, with some emphasis, to the effect that Dumbo certainly is an elephant. Z then repeated the assertion. A introduced into argument Dumbo's trunk and elephant mother. For rebuttal, Z simply restated previous position, "Dumbo is not an elephant." A called in counsel, who advised that since Z was the guest, why not let her say Dumbo is whatever she wants Dumbo to be? Outraged, A said again that Dumbo *was* an elephant, meanwhile beginning to cry and kick the side of her bed as Z, unmoved, looked on.

Court at first refused to hear the case. On reapplication, court ruled that it didn't really matter what kind of animal Dumbo was, now please go to sleep. Decision upheld on appeal.

2. Competition Gone Wrong

A and B, siblings, on car trip, entered ill-advisedly into burping contest. Drinking soda was involved. B said new flavor of soda, tried by him for first time, was pretty good. A replied, "I'll bet it's really not." This later construed as evidence of animus against B. Contest proceeded without further dispute. Burps of A and B roughly equal in quality, volume, etc. After ten minutes, A said she was bored. B then produced outstanding burp, which A let go by without comment. B, noting A's silence, asked her opinion. Still receiving no answer, B said, "Hey, I complimented *your* burps." A replied in a way seen as unforthcoming by B, who then put pressure on A's seat belt until she screamed.

Court pulled over and refused to continue until A and B were silent; both enjoined to remain like that; contest suspended.

3. Ordnance Dispute

B and Y, friends, sitting at campsite picnic table, began discussion of weaponry. Question to be resolved: Can machine guns fire underwater? B inclined to the affirmative, Y to the negative. Advantage seesawed back and forth until Y produced apparent trump, namely, "If machine guns can fire underwater, then why are there spearguns?" Having reached stalemate, question was referred to court for certiorari.

After deliberation, court found greater merit in argument of Y, existence of spearguns being seen in and of itself presumptive of inutility of combustion-propelled projectiles when entire machine gun is underwater. Court made mental note to call gun shop or someplace when home and ask if that actually is correct.

4. The Self-Inflicted Hit

This case involved conflicting complaints presented to court simultaneously. A and B, siblings, were in living room—B on sofa, A in armchair doing math. B was playing with "shark guy," action figure with shark head, big arms, and smaller legs and torso. By manipulating movable shark jaw, B was causing shark guy to sing "Jingle Bells" with first consonants of words replaced, i.e., "Bingle bells, bingle bells, bingle ball be bay," "Dingle dells, dingle dells, dingle dall de day," etc. A requested that B stop. B's response was to make shark guy repeat, through crude ventriloquism and jaw motions, words just spoken by A. Becoming angry, A pretended to hurl math notebook at B. B, not understanding that gesture was merely a feint, quickly lifted his arm to ward off anticipated blow, resulting in unintentional jab to own forehead with pointed end of shark guy. Howling in pain, B then hurled shark guy at A, striking her on wrist. Both immediately sought redress at court.

Here we have a more complex question in kid jurisprudence; that is, how does the "Always use words, not hitting" rule apply to fake or threatened blows, especially when the putative victim's response itself results in harm? Or, in other words, what blame if any accrues to A for a mere gesture that, as she claims, she had no intention of following through? B, representing himself, argued that he had every reason to believe the threat was real, and indicated as corroboration a large bruise below right kneecap, which he claimed was result of A kicking him earlier with field-hockey shoe. On redirect, A said that she did not even *have* field-hockey shoes, because practice had just started and she hadn't gotten them yet. These remarks were followed with animadversions against B beyond scope of discussion.

Fed up, court cut Gordian knot by sending A and B to opposite corners; five minutes for every subsequent remark.

Before sentencing, as well as during and after, court admonished both A and B for their conduct, which he described as the worst seen all afternoon. Court asked if they had any idea how damaging their acts were for society when he was forced to close the door of his basement office so as not to hear their disruption, and then had to get off the phone in the middle of an important call with a client, to whom he was trying to sell half a million dollars of term life insurance, because they came bursting in on him when they had been specifically told not to interrupt until six o'clock. Court asked if A and B would like to make large income necessary to pay the mortgage themselves, and, if not, would they be willing to move to a shack because they had created so much trouble and destroyed the business of the person who fed, sheltered, and clothed them. Court asked how they would like that.

B expressed remorse, had sentence shortened; remanded to video games. A, unrepentant, referred to court as "a big fat hypocrite"; sentence to be continued indefinitely.

5. Birthday-Party Plan

To party for eleventh birthday, B, the celebrant, invited guests D, E, F, G, H, I, and Y. Sodas in refrigerator, cash on counter to pay pizza deliveryman. Court adjourned to third-floor storage room with mattress, food. Closed door tightly. Disregarded sounds of crashing, breakage, screams. Let real court sort it out.

Here to Tell You

There were times that Dad's pranks bordered on cruelty. One of his oil-company workers, a one-legged man he nicknamed "Crip" Smith, complained about everything. Dad and Crip's co-workers got tired of the old man's belly-aching and decided to take revenge. One morning Crip called in sick and Dad volunteered to send by lunch to his grateful but suspicious employee. Dad and his chums caught Crip's old black tomcat, killed it, skinned it, and cooked it in the kitchen of one of Dad's little restaurants. They called it squirrel meat and delivered it to Crip on a linen-covered tray. When Crip returned to work the next morning, Dad and his co-conspirators asked him how he liked his meal. They knew he would complain even about a free home-cooked lunch, and when Crip called it "the toughest squir-rel meat" he had ever eaten, they were glad to tell him why.

—The Reverend Jerry Falwell, *Strength for the Journey: An Autobiography*

There were times that Dad's pranks bordered on what your out-of-control activist judges might call felonies. One of his employees was an effeminate fellow he

nicknamed "Sissybritches" Jones, who had a live-in male homosexual companion for the purposes of sodomy. Ol' Sissy
mentioned one day that since he and this guy he did sodomy
with had been together for years, they had decided to go ahead
and get married. Well, that did it, and so Dad and his friends
decided to take revenge. This sodomite couple had an old
black golden retriever, and because it was old it didn't matter if
it died. Dad and the other dads killed it, doused it with
kerosene, set it on fire, hung it up in automobile headlights for
a while, and then served it as dog meat on linen-covered trays
in their little restaurants. When Sissy and the other one came
around afterward and complained, Dad and his squad were
happy to let them in on the joke. Then they shot and killed
them both.

Of course, I'm exaggerating a little bit here. Every good
story gets exaggerated some in the retelling, and there's nothing
wrong with that. I seem to recall that the two men were not
actually shot and killed, or not at that time. But I think the underlying point of the story remains the same, and it is this:
First, we sometimes forget how much humor there is in the
Bible. The Bible is full of wonderful, earthy humor, if not on
every page, at least on many pages, particularly in the Letters of
Paul. And, second, we should never lose sight of the fact that
Jesus said—get out your Bibles, it's Matthew 10, verse 34—he
said, "I have come not to bring peace, but a sword."

Note that Jesus does not say he came to bring a dagger, or
a wooden club with pointed spikes in it. He specifies a sword.
Why does he do that? Probably because the sword was the
most advanced weapon of Jesus' day. And if we transpose this
saying into our own era, if we wanted a weapon, none of us

would be likely to reach for a sword. The verse could perhaps be better understood in our terms if it referred not to a sword but to an automatic rifle or shotgun sold out of the trunk of a person's car in a lumber-company parking lot in Dothan, Alabama. When we see it like that, we have a better idea of what Jesus was trying to say.

Now, some of the so-called cultural elites in Hollywood and Washington and Raleigh-Durham want to tell us that our long-standing traditions have become somehow unfashionable in the modern world. And don't kid yourselves—when they say that, they're really telling us they're right and we're wrong. They'll say, for example, that you can't blow up a bag of kittens with a shotgun, just because they themselves never did it for a harmless prank when they were young. Then these folks want to turn around and put their values, or lack of values, on everybody else.

Once again, the answer I have for them is simple: Go back to your Bible. In the very first book, first chapter, twenty-sixth verse—read along with me—it says God gave man, quote, "dominion over the fish of the sea, and over the birds of the air, and over all living things on the earth," unquote. What does this mean? If you said that it means you can bury an old black Chihuahua up to its neck in your yard and run over its head with a lawn mower, then you have been paying attention, because you are exactly correct. The key is that little word "dominion." When God uses that word, he is saying, in essence, man can do to the beasts of the earth whatever he wants or feels like at any particular time.

This is especially true, by the way, regarding cats. I happen not to be fond of cats, and that includes secular-humanist cat-like dogs such as Chihuahuas and golden retrievers. This is just a personal preference that I and most of my fellow pastors share. But when I or any other pastor am asked to perform a marriage of homosexual cats, or of homosexual cat-owning people—well, then I think the hour has come for a scourging of wickedness such as God used to do in the biblical lands. I know you all are familiar with the story of the old black tom-cat and the one-legged newlywed lesbian couple from Massachusetts. If you'd be interested to study it further, there's a copy of it on the pink sheet in your bulletin insert. After you read it, you will see several phone numbers at the bottom that you can call.

But that's not what I'm here to talk to you about today. No, it isn't. I am here to tell you that I have never in my life been happier than I am right now. This evening, I actually shed tears of joy at the recent success of our efforts. And as I wept, I also danced a little bit, not lewdly like on MTV, but with a couple crossover steps and a godly kind of hop, I felt so blessed. What miracles have been achieved!

Then I strutted for a while, and gave myself high fives in the full-length mirror in my office in the rectory. My son heard me and he came in, and we did some complicated handshakes that I could share with you all if you would like to learn them. Oh, last November was glorious for those who care, as we do, about the traditional, nonhomosexual, one-man-and-one-woman-with-children-whose-paternity-can-be-verified family! (And by that I mean, of course, a family in which *both* the man *and* the woman were *born* a man and a woman, and can prove it—that is, they are still exactly the same sex as they were when

they were born, and haven't had any of those operations that
are all the rage, I'm told.)

By now, it may be obvious to many of you that I'm on the
verge of hysteria. I split the back of my jacket in my gyrations
before I came out here—those of you behind me would be
able to see it if I weren't wearing this beautiful robe. Friends,
remember our constitutional Federal Marriage Amendment!
We have got to make Congress pass that thing! I believe in my
soul that we will. And, before we do, we better remember to
put in a couple of sentences about the requirement that you be
born a man or a woman, et cetera. I honestly thought of that
only just now.

Oh, I feel an unusual presence of administering angels.
Truly the spirit has descended upon us tonight. I want you all
to bow your heads, and take out your Palm Pilots and Black-
Berrys and cell phones and laptops, and then work and work
them with all your strength, until the kingdom of us begins to
appear.

Chinese Arithmetic

In the event of an erection that persists longer than four hours, the patient should seek immediate medical assistance.

—Precautionary statement in pharmaceutical ad

Sept. 8, 1963, 8:45 a.m.–June 14, 1964, 3:30 p.m. (eighth grade). Debbie Avery, Cammie Flanders, Laurel Gainer, Charmaine Day, Diane Persico, Nancy Thiel, Gail Zobel, Doreen McConaghey. Discomfort in classroom approaching agony. Homeopathic remedies tried.

July 19, 1967, 9:38 p.m.–Oct. 12, 1968, 7:10 p.m. Dating Stacie Rasmussen. Lumbar manipulation partially successful.

Sept. 25, 1969, 5:16 p.m.–sometime in the mid-1970s (college; penumbra of the 1960s). Body painting; girl in art-supply store in Cambridge; photo spread in *Evergreen Review*, etc. Hindu water treatment relatively useless.

May 12, 1977, 10:18 p.m.–May 13, 1977, 11:30 a.m. Anne Lenhart in leather skirt at party on Broome Street. Severe indisposition; patient able to walk only while bent over and moaning. "Talking cure" ineffective.

April 4, 1978, 9:30 p.m.–April 5, 1978, 1:17 a.m. Sudden

sharp onset as a result of watching program *Maude* on TV (Adrienne Barbeau). Afflicted individual turned off set, tried to rest quietly. Swiss astringents a last resort.

Oct. 10, 1978, 9:00 a.m.–Oct. 10, 1978, 4:00 p.m. Painful recurrence while attempting to take LSAT exam (sound of test monitor's hosiery). Reichian orgone-box therapy made things worse.

In subsequent years of adulthood and middle age, sufferer accomodated chronic condition as best he could. Advent of women's fashion craze for extremely tight, low-slung jeans began a difficult period in the case history. Subject had to remain seated almost all the time. Chafing, pain, and occasional loss of verbal and motor skills affected job performance and lifestyle. Then they started wearing those *thong* dealies that are visible in back above the belt line. Unable to cope, patient finally presented at clinic for treatment with classic 24/7 stiffy.

Initial diagnostic exam showed patient's condition rated a code blue on the Guccione hardness-tumescence continuum, at a level described as "harder than Chinese arithmetic"—in other words, a major hard wiener, bearing more surface tension p.s.i. than the standard semi-flaccid routney (as erectographers call it), or than the ordinary, garden-variety boner. Characteristic "pup-tent" effect could be clearly seen when patient finally took hands out of pants pockets. In describing sensations accompanying the disorder, patient used terms frequently associated with it, such as "Oh, ow, ouch, why me? Salma Hayek, girl in the vodka ad, photo of Mrs. Jason Kidd in the *News*, please spare me, Kylie Minogue, oh Jesus," and so on.

Clinicians determined main cause of problem was patient being incredible horn-dog. Asked if he could think about anything else for God's sake for just a minute or two if possible, he replied that he could not. CT brain scan administered forty-eight hours after admittance showed that to be correct. Every cortex and all cognitive functions of patient's brain were occupied with images of J. Lo, and with one scene in particular from her movie *Maid in Manhattan*, which he had recently watched on an airplane without the sound.

J. Lo herself was summoned to clinic and met with patient in observation booth on the grounds. She explained to patient that her movies and CD covers, and the short video of Ben Affleck rubbing suntan lotion on her, were intended for entertainment purposes only, and not as substitute for mature relationship with appropriate partner probably very different from her. Upon departure, she gave patient autographed full-length publicity still, which unfortunately caused him to fall into anaphylactic shock aggravated by drastic worsening of condition. Later brought back to consciousness with IV drip of adreno-eutopophane (120 cc); returned to room.

During first trimester of aggressive medication and treatment, patient showed no change. Second trimester: also no change. Third trimester: slight improvement, later attributed to errors in data caused by faulty instrumentation. Fourth trimester: patient fitted with special clothing and encouraged to mingle in society. Condition unchanged.

On a personal note, it grieved doctors and staff to witness patient's continued disability and yet be unable to help this middle-aged individual, who was, after all, merely attempting to live life while achingly, bakingly inflamed. On good days, some slight improvement might be detected; but then Nurse Randi or Nurse Amber, fairly bursting from her starched nurse's whites, would walk by his room on a nursely errand, and progress would be lost.

In the end, regrettably, nothing could be done for this man. Even the most advanced medical science in the most technologically advanced country in the world has its limits. After eighteen months, patient's insurer refused to pay further costs, and dropped him from the rolls. Burdened with undeniable pre- and post-existing condition, patient was turned down for all other coverage. At present, he is talking on the phone once a week to a paramedic in Bengal who assures him that his disorder will inevitably slowly reverse itself as the body weakens with age. Patient is also promised that any number of illnesses he can reasonably anticipate contracting in the course of time are known to have deflationary and disinflammatory effects. Patient is happily expecting to be relieved at last when he crawls into a nice cold grave.

Square One

*C*orrection: In last week's newsletter, the title of our lead article, "THE DEMOCRATS: HERE DO WE GO FROM WHERE?" contained errors caused by faulty typesetting. We at Democratic Party headquarters deeply regret any misunderstanding this caused. The correct title should have read, "THE DEMOCRATS: DO WE WHERE GO HERE FROM IS THIS RIGHT LORENZO?"

Also, in the first column of the article a paragraph was left out because of somebody's lunch being on it. Without this part, some of the fine points of the author's argument were lost. The omitted paragraph is as follows:

And while I'm tipping over the applecart, I might as well voice another tentative possible caveat about the president that may well bear looking into. It's simply that the way President Bush acts sometimes might make people in foreign countries not like us. With his swaggering, "cowboy" behavior, the president might alienate some of the Europeans, in particular, who as we know have a proud culture of their own. Certainly even a skeptic will concede that could conceivably occur. I agree that most of the countries in question are awfully far away, as a quick glance at an atlas will attest. You will get no argument from me on that. So, you say, what is there to worry about? You may well be right. Actually, this may not be the problem I thought it was.

Another important paragraph in the article was dropped because we don't exactly know why. In it the author mounted a strongly worded criticism of the Republican administration that did not even spare those at the very top. Some readers may have thought that the lines had been cut deliberately because the editors bowed to official pressure, but this is not the case. We will now run the paragraph herewith just as it appeared in the original:

During the last presidential debate, I am told, President Bush referred to "the Internets" (plural). When I heard of this mistake, I had to laugh, for two reasons. First, because it tended to confirm what I have begun to suspect—namely, that the president possesses an intellect that is sometimes less than first-rate (disrespectful as such a statement may sound). Secondly, I got a kick out of President Bush's unconscious betrayal of his unfamiliarity with the new technology. The Internet (not "nets," please note) is *the* great modern communication tool; in addition, it offers a large amount of information at one's fingertips.

We are aware that the above opinions may anger some readers. We apologize. If we get enough negative response, the next time we see the author we will mention to him that he should soften his arguments (especially where he implies that Bush isn't smart). Because we Democrats are also democrats with a small *d*, we carefully value the wishes of each individual, even those with whom we don't agree, in the spirit of bipartisanship.

As we were remarking to Jane Fonda the other day, our party has fallen woefully out of touch with the feelings of average Americans. The author mentioned this point in the newsletter article, but not enough, and we would like to emphasize it even more. Quite simply, in 2004 we forgot our roots as Democrats. We forgot that ordinary people share the same basic desires. They want better lives for themselves and their children; they want jobs, and decent pay for honest work; and they want drug companies not to be sued for selling medicines that cause brain damage—aspirations common to people all over America and, indeed, all over the world.

Nor was that the limit of our failings. The article didn't go into the worst of them, because the author was probably scared to. But they're going to come out sooner or later, so why hide the facts anymore? During the 2004 campaign, a great many of us Democrats drank—heavily. We smoked, also. The air in the Kerry campaign bus would make your eyes tear. Reporters didn't mention this, because the Democratic National Committee begged them not to. Also, we shoplifted a lot of stuff. Ask storekeepers in Boston what it was like during the convention, when, God forgive us, we picked those poor jerks clean. The motorcycle Kerry rode, in those photos? Stolen from a guy. He had outstanding warrants, so he didn't go to the police.

On top of that, we were really horrible to our spouses.

While engaged in the campaign, we called home every night—not to ask our husband or wife how his or her day had been but, rather, to whine and moan about how tired *we* were, and how *hard* we were working, and how *mean* Teresa Heinz Kerry had been to us, and how we hadn't had anything to eat since yesterday but a *bagel*, and how the foam-rubber pillows in the motel aggravated our *allergies*, and boohoohoo wretched miserable *us*, without asking one single question of our long-suffering husband or wife, who was keeping everything together at home, dealing with kids and homework and lessons and exterminators and mildew guys, and he or she couldn't even point out our incredible selfishness because that would be descending to our level and *someone* had to be the grown-up or the whole situation would shatter into a million pieces. And all the while that we were going on like five-year-olds, the ordinary Americans whom we didn't and don't know the feelings of were standing not ten feet away from us in the lobby talking to Karl Rove.

Then, when it would have done us some actual political *good* to cry, what did we do? We clammed up. Sure, a couple of senators almost wept while voting in favor of the war in Iraq, and Kerry managed a sniffle or two during the campaign. We took only hesitant steps, when the situation called for boldness. The country needed to see Kerry really turn on the waterworks, blubbering unashamedly and dabbing his eyes with his necktie and pulling out a hankie the size of a laundry bag and blowing a heartfelt, robust honk to show he wasn't aloof. We could have reached out like that to people, but we missed our chance.

Look, we're going to level with you. (And this goes beyond

the article we were doing corrections for, messed up as it was. Forget about the article now—it's not that important.) We Democrats are a complete disaster. We have made a hash of our party and of our lives—yes, a stinky, ten-day-old corned-beef hash that even the cat won't touch. Back to square one. Sheep-dip and apple butter. *Help us, please!* On our wrist is a MedicAlert bracelet with name, affiliation, and Donald Rumsfeld's telephone number. Rummy—Condi, whoever—we surrender! Where do we sign? We're facedown on the pavement, arms and legs spread. You want to destroy the environment? We never noticed it that much anyway. Abortion? Do as you think best. Social Security? Hey, you're the man—we just live here. Evolution? It *doesn't* make much sense, now that you mention it. Seventeen thousand a year at Wal-Mart suits us fine. Mind if we help ourselves to these hors d'oeuvres?

It is interesting to note that our Democratic Party has traditionally done better in years beginning with an *R*. I can't think of any examples of this right now, but I know I've come across it in the literature. Franklin Roosevelt, of course, is the exception that proves the rule, being a Republican. Or maybe a Democrat—I forget which. At any rate, he had to be one or the other because the Whig Party had been dissolved by then. History is a fascinating thing. The other day I was reading an old book and it said that back in the nineteen-hundreds there was another president named Bush. The only difference between

*

Hello, I'm Jack Welch. Since buying the Democratic Party two months ago, I have had to fire literally thousands of people like those responsible for the above. I include their babblings here only as an example of the kind of incompetence, waste, and mismanagement that will no longer be tolerated in the Democratic Party. The new Democratic Party will be lean and . . . what's the other thing? Goes with "lean"? Oh, hell, you know. Rhymes with it. I *know* it, goddamn it! Why can't I think of it? Schumer! *Schumer!* Get your lazy butt in here! Now, goddamn it, Schumer, I want you to find whoever is responsible for my not knowing what rhymes with "lean" and fire his behind out the door. Tell him just get his stuff and get out. Call security and make sure he doesn't take any office supplies.

That's the kind of no-nonsense approach you can expect in the new, non-incompetent Democratic Party with me in charge. During the coming months, keep your eyes and ears open for many changes. There will be an attractive new logo, plus illustrative icons, online banking, and other innovations. A new Democratic Party, fit to compete in the environment it has to compete in. And—best of all—run by me.

From now on, send all contributions to my place in New York.

Pensées d'Automne

It's fall again, and time for putting on my big, heavy boots and stomping on acorns. My boot of choice is a shin-high Danner Foothill model with a Vibram sole and a hard rubber heel a good inch and a quarter tall. Not many acorns will stand up to these fellows. The heel is the important part. Like a golf club or a tennis racket, each heel has a sweet spot that sends a feeling of rightness through your whole body when the acorn is struck properly. This spot is in the middle of the heel, toward the back, in line with the center of the leg coming down into the boot. Hit a single acorn just so and you get a satisfying, shivery tingling between the shoulder blades. Hit a series of acorns, first right, then left, then right, and so on as long as the random distribution of acorns on the sidewalk permits, each acorn struck square on the sweet spot, *crunch, crunch, crunch*, never breaking stride—well, that's what you're looking for.

The town in suburban New Jersey where I live is ideal for doing this. Hundreds of oak trees, tens of thousands of acorns. Right about now the acorns are everywhere, piling up on the sidewalks and along the curbs, raining down and bouncing off people's heads when the wind blows. Freshly fallen ones are rich autumnal shades of Rembrandt brown or dark olive (among others), and their pale tops, just separated from their cupules, are clean as a new sheet of stationery. The small brown acorns come from the pin oak, and the larger olive acorns from the red oak. The larger acorn compresses underfoot with a meaty, splintery impact that leaves a roughly circular flattened self about the size of a dollar pancake. The smaller acorn, early in the season, when still at prime ripeness, gives off when stomped a sharp little report like a shot from a cap pistol. Sometimes I prefer the one, sometimes the other.

I am not the only person around here who stomps on acorns, though I'm probably the only adult. In the mornings, I see schoolchildren bent like Sherpas under their enormous backpacks nevertheless veering back and forth to stomp any available acorn in their paths. There are usually not many un-stomped acorns in the vicinity of schools. Fortunately, the town has miles of slate sidewalks, which are lightly traveled. The sidewalk plates tilt this way and that over the tree roots, and many pedestrians and joggers and people pushing baby strollers prefer to use the smoother street pavement beside the curb—ergo, more acorns for me. Nobody seems to notice what I'm doing or pay me any mind. Maybe it just looks as if I'm walking erratically. Once, as I came stomping to a cross-walk, a woman on the passenger side of a big car waiting at the light rolled her window partway down and appeared to give me a nervous wave. When I approached closer, however, I saw that she had just opened a pack of cigarettes and was trying to get rid of the torn-off cellophane wrap, which had stuck to the ends of her fingers by static electricity.

This isn't stem-cell research—it's stomping on acorns. As

Joe Garagiola, the sports announcer, used to say, "You don't want to be thinking too much out there." I admit that for a while I went at this with the mistaken notion that I was "working out frustrations." That was wrong, a too simple gloss and scrim over urges that go much deeper. Stomping on things that can be stomped on is an activity that humans have always done, whether frustrated or no. There's an acorn; you step on it. Splat. 'Nuff said.

True, it's hard to stay centered in the moment like that every second. There are distractions—the squirrels, for example, which (no doubt thanks to the acorns) infest the town. I know that Americans are now the fattest people on earth, but have you taken a look recently at American animals? Starlings and seagulls and raccoons have gotten so fat they can hardly move. Our town has squirrels with white bellies as broad across, proportionately, as Pavarotti's. These moguls chew holes at their leisure in plastic garbage-can lids, taking what they like from within. I sometimes see them waddling along with entire Eggo toaster waffles in their mouths. Just before acorn season, their binge time, they begin to rifle the upper oak branches as frantically as if they'd just quit smoking.

To be honest, I should lose some weight myself. That is one reason I started this walking to begin with. The same almost visible dread pursues me as it does my jogging neighbors, the grave continuously opening behind our heels. Stomp, stomp, stomp! Get away from me! And, speaking of that, do you have any idea what I pay for health insurance? It's incredible. There've been years in which the premiums went up 34 percent. A while ago I saw in the business section of the *News* an article about CIGNA, the HMO we belonged to, which said that the company earned $290 million, or $2.06 a share, in the fourth quarter of 2003. For shareholders, this was an encouraging increase on the $47 million, or thirty-three cents a share, earned the year before. CIGNA planned to make even more money by cutting three thousand jobs and $300 million in expenses, the article said. The real point of the article was to report that a court had approved, and CIGNA had agreed to pay, a $540 million settlement owed to doctors for "systematically" underpaying them. Of course, we want the shareholders to make money, and it's always good to cut the deadwood from the staff, but for God's sake don't do anything as foolish and fiscally unsound as paying *doctors* . . .

I hate even to think about CIGNA. Fall into a vexation-filled CIGNA reverie and you lose your concentration, go off your game, and start to mis-stomp acorns, so that instead of neatly flattening, they squirt out from under your heel unstomped, or partly stomped, and bounce woundedly away. That is an awful feeling. Theologians have defined sin as "apartness from God," but I think that sin, in practical terms, is a lot like the jarring, jangling wrongness of the wrongly hit baseball or mis-stomped acorn—a kind of teeth-grinding, bone-deep discord that makes the very keelson of the universe vibrate off-key.

The mis-stomped acorn, however, may explain an unexpected phenomenon of nature I learned about the other day. I was reading a book about the ice ages—I like books about America before anyone was here, even Indians; I think a good book would be called *America Before Anyone*—and the author was describing the reforestation of land after the ice caps receded, and she said that different species of trees advanced at different rates. Maples, with their wind-dispersed seeds, advanced at a rate of 200 meters a year, while oaks, despite their heavier, non-wind-dispersed acorns, reoccupied formerly glaciated lands at a rate of 350 meters a year. The oak forests, in other words, moved almost twice as fast as the maple forests. Clearly, some outside agents had to be at work. How else could oaks go that fast except for your wandering post-ice-age mammals nudging or pushing or perhaps even inaccurately stomping on acorns, and helping them along? The hoof comes down, the partly stepped-on acorn shoots out, and the old play-by-the-rules maple gets left behind.

Soon, our leaves and acorns will be raked and leaf-blown into heaps along the curb. Last week I was walking (not, for that moment, stomping) in my neighborhood and an old man raking leaves by the sidewalk stopped and turned to me and said, "I've been doing this all my life." Special loaders, beeping as they back up, will come and collect the heaps and pile them into trucks, and the great mass of leaves and shattered or still unshattered acorns—a huge harvest—will be dumped at a Meadowlands compost site. We live surrounded by crazy, unused bounty, as in the smell of our never-grazed lawns after they are mown: because wild onions often grow in the grass, that mowed-lawn smell is not just delicious but gourmet.

When the president of Venezuela, Hugo Chávez, was in New York City a few weeks ago for a meeting at the United Nations, he told a *News* reporter that he had counted automobiles as he rode in from J.F.K. Airport. "Out of every 100 cars I saw on the road, 99 had only one person in the car . . . This planet cannot sustain that mode of life," Chávez said. He also told the reporter that his favorite American writer was Noam

Chomsky. Chávez's remarks interested me, so I went to hear him speak at a community center at 170th Street and Jerome Avenue, in the South Bronx. There he announced that Venezuela will sell oil at below-market price to poor neighborhoods, beginning with the South Bronx, this winter. I know that only secondhand, however; because of threats against Chávez's life from a leading American evangelist, security at the event was tight and I did not get in.

It's been unusually hard to keep my mind on my stomping this fall. That's a shame, too, because toward the end of the season there's always a final acorn bonanza, and fresh ones rustle constantly through the leaves on their way down, and bounce satisfyingly, and roll into a pattern along the sidewalk that I couldn't improve on if I placed them there myself. I'm occasionally able to stomp a dozen or fourteen in a row under alternate feet in perfect, uninterrupted sequence, like a pool shark running the table. And sometimes, to make sure my attention stays on my work, I accompany my stomping with simple, expressive chants: I recite the individual letters in "CIGNA," with an acorn stomped decisively after each letter; or, for a while, I couldn't help trying the famous sentence about Brownie, coming down extra hard on ". . . heckuva job!" (stomp).

One important key, I've found, is not to read the paper before going on a stomp; don't read, for example, the story about Senate Majority Leader Bill Frist's sale of stock in the hospital chain his family founded, a sale that brought Senator Frist an undisclosed number of dollars, and which was followed very shortly thereafter (just his luck) by a 9 percent drop in the stock's market value in a single day, after the release of a disappointing earnings report. This company, called HCA, had previously climbed back to a respectable share price after reaching a sorry low five years ago, when its officers pleaded guilty to fourteen criminal counts of Medicare fraud and paying kickbacks, and paid $1.7 billion in penalties and fines. One point seven billion! CIGNA, tagged for a measly half a billion and change, must be a timid, effete, small-time enterprise not to do any better than that!

And, of course, all this puts me in another vexatious CIGNA fret, which becomes a tortured general-objections fret, and my stomping accuracy goes all to hell, and the glories of the New Jersey fall pass invisibly by.

Caught

A crafty coyote . . . led the law on a two-day chase through Central Park before he was brought down yesterday by a sharpshooter with a tranquilizer gun . . . The coyote [was] nicknamed Hal because he was spotted near the Hallett Nature Sanctuary . . . "This is New York, and I would suggest that the coyote may have had more problems than the rest of us," Mayor Bloomberg said.

—*Daily News*, March 23, 2006

Nobody knows how Hal got into Central Park. But he wasn't the first. A coyote was found there in 1999 . . . Otis, the coyote captured in Central Park in 1999, was brought to the Queens Zoo where he still lives.

—*Daily News*, March 24, 2006

Hal, the crafty Central Park coyote, mysteriously died Thursday night—just as he was set to return to the wild, officials said . . . The young coyote . . . stopped breathing as his ears were being tagged at a Putnam County forest . . . "It's one of the saddest and hardest things we have had to deal with as wildlife rehabilitators," said Rebecca Asman, a city cop who took Hal in after his capture. "Hopefully something can be learned from this so there can be better outcomes for this very misunderstood animal."

—*Daily News*, April 1, 2006

I f you're really interested in hearing all this, you probably first want to know where I was whelped, and what my parents' dumb burrow was like, and how they started me out hunting field mice, and all the *Call of the Wild* kind of crap, but I'd really rather not go into it, if that's all right with you. It's not that I don't have the time, residing here in Queens and all, where I can rest up conveniently, and not be a hazard to the joggers and the ducks and so on. In Queens, I really have quite a free schedule, between feedings, and pacing back and forth, which I don't really have to do but I do it anyway, because the little kids seem to enjoy it, and I feel it is expected of me. One so-called biographical fact I will mention, just because I find the whole business so damn aggravating, is that before I was here I did not have a name—not Otis, not anything—and I wish I didn't have one now. It's really not coyote-like. To have a name at all, that is, let alone Otis. I guess you'd probably have to be a coyote to know what I mean.

The thing I want to tell you about isn't my poor deprived growing up or anything like that, but a bunch of stuff that happened to me a long while ago when I first came to New York City, which you may have heard a little bit about if you were the kind of person who was reading the newspapers around then. What made me think of it was, recently I was at my water dish, and I saw this crazy picture that looked sort of like me, on the newspaper lining this stupid wire-mesh floor of the cage under the dish, I mean. That picture was almost like I was looking in a goddamn mirror, I swear to God. Right on the front page was this coyote, who could even be my own dumb little brother for all I know, standing on some rocks, and you can see some water next to him, some grass and whatnot growing alongside, and he's looking straight up at the photographer with this particular expression in his eyes—not a dopey expression, but sort of the opposite of dopey, you might say. Like what he's *looking* at is dopey; it's hard to describe. And, as he's looking, the coyote is licking his nose with his tongue. The tongue kind of curls up over his nose, and you can tell he's about to start down the right side of his muzzle, and lick there, too. I couldn't believe it when I noticed that. I've done that myself only about a couple of hundred thousand times. It's a habit I have.

Probably he's just taken a drink of the water he's standing next to, in the picture, I mean. That's the reason he's licking his nose. After you drink, you'll find there's almost always a few drops of water hanging from the end of your nose, which can be rather irritating, believe me. And in the meantime this photographer starts to snap, from a goddamn tree limb, maybe even hanging by his heels or something, probably all red in the face after running full speed for about eighty miles trying to find the coyote, photo equipment and straps and all hanging down and dangling everywhere from the tree while the camera is making these very upsetting *snap snap snap snap snap* sounds. This variety of sound also happens to be very terrifying to ducks, by the way.

You see, I can tell, from my own personal experience, almost exactly where the coyote is standing. It's in the park by the pond where they have an absolutely enormous amount of ducks. That happens to be just about my favorite place in the whole city, it really is. Not many people are aware that New York has a great number of very fat and slow ducks that just sort of go gobbling along enjoying themselves right near the shoreline, not far away out in the middle where a bunch of swimming would be required. And then this photographer comes along snapping photos and cracking tree limbs and causing pieces of bark to fall in the water, scaring the ducks away.

But that's not exactly the stuff I started to tell you about, though—I mean the stuff that happened to me a few years back that I mentioned before. In my case, with the particular events involving myself and ducks and so on, my problems, if you want to call them that, started when I got kind of turned around geographically—I've always had the crappiest sense of direction, it's a terrible flaw for someone in my occupation. Suddenly I was about halfway lost and running all over on extremely hard ground with cars and buildings and all that, never even a bush where I could crawl in and take a breather, and sometimes people were shouting at me. Then high up in the air I saw a couple of ducks, a welcome sight, not that these were the fattest or the closest ducks in the world, you understand, but still it kind of improved my mood just seeing them there.

The thing about ducks flying in the air is, they can't stay there forever—they have to come down. As a coyote you learn this fact pretty early on, trust me. And, when they do come down, 99 percent of the time it's a pond or lake-type area, and, if you're lucky, fairly near the bank, as I pointed out before. So

I kept an eye on the general direction these ducks seemed to be going, and I went that way myself, with a lot more running, and being shouted at, and some dodging around cars that I really could have done without, quite frankly. Then I saw a lot of trees, and a stone wall that I kind of leaped over, and then I was in the park, where it's much more relaxing, if you tend to be excitable, which I sometimes am.

Pretty soon I saw some water up ahead, and I could tell it was a pond, and, sure enough, ducks were on it. I don't know if it was the same ducks I saw flying earlier, but it could have been. I don't know that much about the individual ducks, to be perfectly honest, because they all kind of blend together for me. Really, I have never seen such an incredible bonanza of ducks as were in that pond, and even geese and a few goofy swans with those long necks and whatnot, like a coyote's crazy dream. Right away I decided this was my favorite place ever, as I mentioned previously. I kind of strolled over to it in a quiet way, around on the other side of the rocks, so as not to get them all flustered and unhappy. I sat back in the rocks and bushes and enjoyed the scenery and finally let my heart go back to a more normal rate of speed for a change.

But if you're really partial to ducks, like I am, you want to do more than just watch them, so pretty soon I began creeping up using this special method that I have, with my knees bent and my stomach practically brushing the ground. It looks kind of strange, but it's effective as hell. The only drawback when I do that is sometimes I forget about my tail, and the stupid thing won't stay down. That's something I know I have to work on, I really do. Anyway, I must've forgotten, and my tail must've gone up, and someone must've seen it. All at once there was yelling, and people pointing, so I quickly decided to go for a kind of unobtrusive stroll someplace far away. But then I noticed a car was following me, and another car, and another, and then goddamn helicopters, if you can believe it, and there were people on one side of me, and when I turned there were more over there. Well, I won't exhaust you with all the stupid details. I think they probably shot me with one of those tranquilizer-dart jobs. I had a hell of a headache afterward, I can tell you that.

I'd like to meet that other coyote, the one whose picture I saw, and tell him I really sympathize with what he's dealing with at the duck pond. Not to get all sappy or anything, but my heart kind of goes out to the poor slob. I feel like if I could give him any helpful advice, which I probably can't ever do because there's no chance I'd ever actually meet up with him or anything—but if I did, I'd tell him to stay as far from the ducks as he possibly can. I know it goes against common sense, but these people here don't want coyotes near the ducks at all. It's not like anybody would miss one or two of them, they have so many. Maybe these people have a duck fetish or something. Maybe it's a whole city full of goddamn duck worshippers— don't ask me. Anyway, just take my word for it, leaving their precious goddamn ducks alone is definitely the best policy.

What the hell, I'll even go further than that and say, Don't go anywhere near the whole dumb city at all if you can help it, is my advice, but that's my completely frank opinion, so help me God. Maybe I'm an animal with certain problems and all, like they say, but I still think I've learned some halfway brilliant things in my life. If I weren't sort of temporarily stuck here, I'd love to tell him all this junk, and help him out.

Thin Enough

Like many middle-aged suburban fathers, I suffer from a problem I am hesitant to name. Recently, though, I've decided that stating what is wrong with me, and admitting it up front, are essential first steps to a cure. So here goes: For many years now, I have been struggling with anorexia. My physique, well muscled and whipcord thin to all outward appearances, is actually *too* thin—painfully thin, in fact. Another uncomfortable truth I have to face is that my family has been hiding this reality from me. My wife soft-soaps me with comments like "You know, sweetie, you're really not thin at all." The kids chime in with an unhelpful "Actually, we'd be more likely to describe you as fat." I know there's a lot of love in what they say, but let's stop all the lying right now. I am incredibly, incredibly thin, and it's time we noticed what is going on.

I myself participate in the deception sometimes, when I split a pair of trousers or have trouble fitting into an airplane seat. Who am I trying to fool? Much as I might wish it, that is simply not me. The truth is, I am a stick person. For I don't know how long, I have literally starved myself trying to attain a body image that bears no relation to how men actually are. The media hammers this image into our brains every day, but now I begin to understand: I can have the same glasses as Karl Rove, wear my belt like Karl Rove, wave from the insides of car windows like Karl Rove. But I will never *be* Karl Rove, so I might as well quit trying. Even Karl Rove probably can't look as fabulous as Karl Rove. I have martyred myself trying to become a fantasy.

Before I can hope to move on, I have to fix my crazy eating habits. During the height of my dieting mania, I used to torture myself regularly at the all-you-can-eat supper at Country Harvest Buffet. I would serve myself a platter of ribs, macaroni and cheese, potato salad, biscuits, peach cobbler, iced tea, no other dessert besides pie—and that would be all. Compared with the dishes of food still on the buffet table, my portion always appeared pitifully small, not enough to feed a fairly good-sized bird. And since I'm trying to be honest here and confess everything, sometimes after eating even that trifling amount, I would go to the men's room and not throw up, but smoke an expensive cigar until the feeling passed, if it had existed in the first place. Then, ready for more, I'd return to the buffet. I gloried in this punitive regimen as the pounds melted off, but I did not suspect the pathology involved.

So much to go through just for the evanescent pleasure of looking wonderful in a swimsuit! But conforming to others' physical expectations was not all to the good, I found. As I approached my ideal weight, I suffered the painful experience of being the victim of sexual harassment on the job. What made it even more confusing and upsetting was that I am my own boss. On several occasions around the office, I made remarks to myself that were completely out of line. Once by the water cooler I grabbed my buttocks. These hurtful words and actions created an atmosphere in which it was impossible for me to do my work. I have since taken a leave of absence.

I see now that the anorexia contributed to this unfortunate situation in two ways—first, by giving me a physical appearance that was extremely "attractive," in the warped judgment of many (i.e., myself), and, second, by causing nutritional deprivations that broke down moral boundaries, leading me to behave inappropriately toward other individuals (again, myself). I am still undecided about taking legal action, but clearly a lot of soul-searching and emotional sorting out need to be done.

As much of a recovery as I've made so far I owe to an often overlooked wonder drug, alcohol. People drink alcohol for the pleasure and the taste, sometimes forgetting its medicinal properties. Scientists have failed to explain why consumption of alcohol causes an increase in appetite, but I can testify that it does. After four or five glasses of wine, I am able to overcome my usual food finickiness and eat half a Crock-Pot of whatever my wife has made for dinner, and then a couple of baskets of leftover Easter candy. If I sense the appetite starting to flag, I'll open another bottle of wine, make a few phone calls to distant friends or people I went to high school with, start in on a pear tart my sister brought over, listen to music really loud, eat a bunch more Easter candy, fall asleep on the living-room floor, and so forth. Little by little, this careful process has been building the bulk back on.

But I can never relax. Anorexia is a patient and crafty adversary, always waiting for me to stop stuffing myself for the briefest interval so that it can gain another foothold. In the past few months, I've been feeling somewhat safe: I'm of average height, and have managed to attain for extra security a respectable weight of several hundred pounds. Then, just the other morning, I looked in the bathroom mirror and noticed that my head was a bit higher in relation to the towel rack than it had been the day before. Men in their fifties do not commonly go through growth spurts, but apparently that is happening to me. You don't have to be an alarmist to see where it could lead. I keep increasing in height, I reach seven or eight feet, and all my hard-won weight is stretched lengthwise until I'm a grotesque string-bean skeleton again.

Fortunately for me, Hilson's Products has come out with a new, more chocolaty version of their Death by Chocolate ice-cream bar, with chocolate on the outside, then vanilla around mint surrounding a rich real-chocolate core. Even when the mere thought of food makes me ill, I can eat a box of those. Another discovery I've made is the factory trawler ships' Weekly Seafood Specials, where they fly you offshore by helicopter and you choose your own netful of bunker or menhaden or whatever baitfish they're hauling up that day. Doesn't get any fresher than that! Also, I know some people at Archer Daniels Midland who give me access to the corn-syrup silos in Moline, where I can open the spigots and down as much as I feel like—none of this making it into McFlurrys or some such pap—just the real syrup, thick and undiluted and strong. You know what else is not bad? No. 2 heating oil. No. 6 oil is okay, too, but you have to cut the sulfur content of both with a good Australian Shiraz, and that runs up the tab. Sulfur can also be a problem with bituminous coal, which is priced right but involves digestive issues that make it less of a bargain. Anthracite, on the other hand, can be lower in sulfur, but it's very hard on the teeth. Then finish it off with a jolt of pure power right from the grid; just—*zap!* If you like, I can give you the recipes.

I'm still too thin, though. I have robust mini-potbellies behind each elbow, and my forearms are good and stout, but the wrists are looking a little spindly. And I don't like the outside parts of my hands, the way they taper off. I can see the thinness there, waiting to strike. On my ankles, too; I've never been able to do anything with them. They could use another five or ten pounds apiece. I'll have to get the opposite of liposuction done to them. (Who in the world, by the way, would deliberately have perfectly good fat removed and then thrown down the drain?) By now, you're probably having some uncomplimentary thoughts about me. Well, I don't care even a fig for you. Wait a minute—let me see that fig. I just want to look at it. Gimme that.

Downpaging

Check books out of the library instead of buying them . . .
New releases of hard-cover novels cost $25 and more these
days. If you buy just two a month, that's *$600 a year.*
—"Ten Sure Ways to Trim Your Budget," *Daily News*

Polk Benham, St. Marys, Ohio: "Right now, it's costing me forty-five dollars to fill up my 4Runner, which is about two novels. Tough decisions are going to have to be made. I'm used to having a newly released hardcover on the dash of my vehicle, another in the backseat for the kids. At home, we've got a novel in each bedroom, two in the family room, one in the laundry room for my wife when she's down there, and a novella in the john. We go through a couple of dozen novels in a year without even noticing. I hate to say it, but this can't go on."

Mrs. Louise Rodgers, Eau Claire, Wisconsin: "I never owned brand-new hardcovers when I was a girl, and now I want my twin sixteen-year-old boys to enjoy opportunities I didn't have. My boys are like any American teenagers, in that they eat, sleep, and breathe novels. And they don't want the three-dollar used paperback version, either. It's got to be new, mint, original dust jacket, the works. How do you tell a youngster that he can't have that just-released Modern Library edition of the complete Sinclair Lewis he's been dreaming of? But I guess that's what I'm going to have to do; I don't see any other option."

Jules Amthor, Torrance, California: "Let me give you a hypothetical situation: I'm walking down the street, I pass a bookstore, and they have a little table out front with some of the latest novels. I pick one up. The jacket says it's about a male professor of writing who has an affair with a much younger female student. I leaf through the book, and I come across a sentence about the student, who is also very beautiful, sleeping in the passenger seat of a car that the narrator (the professor) is driving, and the student wakes, and stretches, and looks at the professor, and—here's the part that gets me—*the pattern of the car-seat upholstery is still imprinted on her cheek.* Well, there's simply no way I'm not going to buy that book. I can be dead broke, nothing left on the credit cards—doesn't matter. And that's what happens to me, over and over again!"

Mitch Gelman, West Hempstead, New York: "As an accountant, the first thing I tell my clients is 'Get a library card!' Otherwise, you're too subject to temptation, and liable to find yourself in over your head. Few people know that the leading cause of personal bankruptcy in the United States is the 'Clan of the Cave Bear' novels. You overspend on one, and, just when you begin to dig yourself out, the next installment comes along. Public libraries began during the Depression as a government measure against this very problem. They're there for our protection, so we should use them."

Senator Jeff Sessions (R-Alabama): "If every American back in 1950 had quit buying novels and invested money in high-yield bonds, today we would be looking at a savings surplus of several trillion dollars, and Social Security would not be in the mess it's in. Instead, we know what happened—most of the money wound up in the pockets of one unscrupulous novelist, Pearl S. Buck, with the disastrous consequences of which we are too well aware. The fact that that woman never spent a day in jail is a disgrace to the history of our nation. I would ask every American, before you lavish your next paycheck on expensive novels you may not need, consider the other spending choices available. You could expand your cable service, visit a casino, make a political donation, give to a faith-based concern, or put the money in something the brokers call a flort. I think we all know a little bit better how our earnings should be spent than the average novel writer does."

Ms. Mabel Dodge Luhan (decd.), Taos, New Mexico: "Our wasteful consumer society buys, reads, and discards more brand-new hardcover fiction in a single day than the rest of the industrial world combined. I find that statistic staggering."

Parker "Chick" Tones, Sanibel Island, Florida: "As a man greatly favored by fortune, I can tell you the secret of my success in a single word: bookmarks. Everybody's gotta have 'em, someone's gotta make 'em and sell 'em. Understanding that simple economic reality just a tick ahead of my rivals brought me wealth, position, and power. Currently, however, I am very glad to be out of the business and retired. People don't seem to care where they start or stop in a book nowadays, so long as they're reading. They'll mark their place with just their thumb, a magazine blow-in ad, a piece of string. And the minute they finish one novel they toss it aside and start another. I've seen people on the freeway flip through a novel to the denouement, read it, and throw the book out the window. Then they'll swing by a bodega, buy a new novel or two or a dozen, and be on their way. No one bothers to pick up the old novels, so they're scattered all over, as we know, backing up in storm drains. The excess of it appalls me."

Ben Bernanke, Federal Reserve Bank, St. George, Bermuda: "If I may, I would like to return for a moment to the topic of the financial instrument known colloquially as a flort, which was mentioned earlier, because I feel it was insufficiently explained. The term 'flort' is simply a shortened form of 'FLORT,' which is an acronym for a much longer and more complex phrase involving entire words. A flort, in essence, is a type of non-available annuity whereby depositors make a pre-determined contribution every year with the expectation that they will either get it back or not. Usually the latter is the case, in which case, fine. They did not have that much anyway, and no one but them is out anything. In certain instances, however, something else happens, which is that the flort value actually doubles or even quadruples, like Greenspan's did. As if he needed it! There's a guy with the dough! Cheney, too. Plus all the senators—man, are they in the chips! And you know what you never see any of the big-bucks guys do? Buy novels. They learned their lesson, disciplined themselves when they were young. The super-ultra-wealthy never touch the modern novel, thus racking up more than six hundred extra dollars per year, on top of what they're making already. Well, they're not like everybody . . . Now I forget what I was talking about before. Oh, yeah—florts. Thank you."

Melissa S., Manhattan: "Eventually, I was able to cut back on novels to one a month, then half a novel, then just a few pages. As of this week, I have not looked at a novel (except from the library) for eighteen months, knock wood. For the first time, I'm learning what it is to live within a budget. At the end of the month, I'm always surprised to find a positive balance in my checking account—it's nice. Little by little, I've reacquainted myself with my TV. There have been some innovations in the formats of reality shows that I had known nothing about. Every morning now I make it a point to get dressed and go outside. I'm paying more attention to my hair. If I hadn't happened to pick up that copy of the *Daily News* that day, I don't know where I'd be."

How to Operate the Shower Curtain

D ear Guest: The shower curtain in this bathroom has been purchased with care at a reputable "big box" store in order to provide maximum convenience in showering. After you have read these instructions, you will find with a little practice that our shower curtain is as easy to use as the one you have at home.

You'll note that the shower curtain consists of several parts. The top hem, closest to the ceiling, contains a series of regularly spaced holes designed for the insertion of shower-curtain rings. As this part receives much of the everyday strain of usage, it must be handled correctly. Grasp the shower curtain by its leading edge and gently pull until it is flush with the wall. Step into the tub, if you have not already done so. Then take the other edge of shower curtain and cautiously pull it in opposite direction until it, too, adjoins the wall. A little moisture between shower curtain and wall tiles will help curtain to stick.

Keep in mind that normal bathing will cause you unavoidably to bump against the shower curtain, which may cling to you for a moment owing to the natural adhesiveness of water. Some guests find the sensation of wet plastic on their naked flesh upsetting, and overreact to it. Instead, pinch the shower curtain between your thumb and forefinger near where it is adhering to you and simply move away from it until it is disengaged. Then, with the ends of your fingers, push it back to where it is supposed to be.

If shower curtain reattaches itself to you, repeat process above. Under certain atmospheric conditions, a convection effect creates air currents outside shower curtain which will press it against you on all sides no matter what you do. If this happens, stand directly under showerhead until bathroom microclimate stabilizes.

Many guests are surprised to learn that all water pipes in our system run off a single riser. This means that the opening of any hot or cold tap, or the flushing of a toilet, interrupts flow to shower. If you find water becoming extremely hot (or cold), exit tub promptly while using a sweeping motion with one arm to push shower curtain aside.

REMEMBER TO KEEP SHOWER CURTAIN *INSIDE* TUB AT ALL TIMES! Failure to do this may result in baseboard rot, wallpaper mildew, destruction of living-room ceiling below, and possible dripping onto catered refreshments at social event in your honor that you are about to attend. So be careful!

This shower curtain comes equipped with small magnets in the shape of disks which have been sewn into the bottom hem at intervals. These serve no purpose whatsoever and may be ignored. Please do not tamper with them. The vertical lines, or pleats, which you may have wondered about, are there for a simple reason: user safety. If you have to move from the tub fast, as outlined above, the easy accordion-type folding motion of the pleats makes that possible. The gray substance in some of the inner pleat folds is a kind of insignificant mildew, less toxic than what is found on some foreign cheeses.

When detaching shower curtain from clinging to you or when exiting tub during a change in water temperature, bear in mind that there are seventeen mostly empty plastic bottles of shampoo on tub edge next to wall. These bottles have accumulated in this area over time. Many have been set upside down in order to concentrate the last amounts of fluid in their cap mechanisms, and are balanced lightly. Inadvertent contact with a thigh or knee can cause all the bottles to be knocked over and to tumble into the tub or behind it. If this should somehow happen, we ask that you kindly pick the bottles up and put them back in the same order in which you found them. Thank you.

While picking up the bottles, a guest occasionally will lose his or her balance temporarily, and, in even rarer cases, fall. If you find this occurring, remember that panic is the enemy here. Let your body go limp, while reminding yourself that the shower curtain is not designed to bear your weight. Grabbing onto it will only complicate the situation.

If, in a "worst case" scenario, you do take hold of the shower curtain, and the curtain rings tear through the holes in the upper hem as you were warned they might, remain motionless and relaxed in the position in which you come to rest. If subsequently you hear a knock on the bathroom door, respond to any questions by saying either "Fine" or "No, I'm fine." When the questioner goes away, stand up, turn off shower, and lay shower curtain flat on floor and up against tub so you can see the extent of the damage. With a sharp object—

a nail file, a pen, or your teeth—make new holes in top hem next to the ones that tore through.

Now lift shower curtain with both hands and reattach it to shower-curtain rings by unclipping, inserting, and reclipping them. If during this process the shower curtain slides down and again goes onto you, reach behind you to shelf under medicine cabinet, take nail file or curved fingernail scissors, and perform short, brisk slashing jabs on shower curtain to cut it back. It can always be repaired later with safety pins or adhesive tape from your toiletries kit.

At this point, you may prefer to get the shower curtain out of your way entirely by gathering it up with both arms and ripping it down with a sharp yank. Now place it in the waste receptacle next to the john. In order that anyone who might be overhearing you will know that you are still all right, sing "Fat Bottomed Girls," by Queen, as loudly as necessary. While waiting for tub to fill, wedge shower curtain into waste receptacle more firmly by treading it underfoot with a regular high-knee action as if marching in place.

We are happy to have you as our guest. There are many choices you could have made, but you are here, and we appreciate that. Operating the shower curtain is kind of tricky. Nobody is denying that. If you do not wish to deal with it, or if you would rather skip the whole subject for reasons you do not care to reveal, we accept your decision. You did not ask to be born. There is no need ever to touch the shower curtain again. If you would like to receive assistance, pound on the door, weep inconsolably, and someone will be along.

What I Am

One of my jobs around the house is to load and run the dishwasher. I believe I do this job very successfully. The other day I loaded both racks, top and bottom, according to a special method that I have. Then I turned the machine on. As a result of some mishap, during the wash cycle a number of the dishes were broken, including a serving dish with a pattern of leaves and olives which my wife had particularly liked. While unloading the dishwasher, she discovered the breakage, and she brought the pieces of the dish to show me. I expressed sympathy, and then began to describe my method of dishwasher loading. This did not make much headway with her, because she disagrees with my method and in fact has asked me several times not to use it. I kept trying to explain, and in the course of the discussion just for a second she lost control and said something hurtful and unkind. I will not go into details, except to say that she referred to me as an "idiot" (quotation marks mine).

Okay; point taken. Based on some of the things I do and their consequences, her characterization of me is not inaccurate, as far as it goes. What I object to isn't so much that as the terminology employed. Quite simply, "idiot" is not a nice word to call somebody, and I find myself asking, as Mr. Welch did of Senator Joseph McCarthy, "Have you no sense of decency, sir?" Throughout my life, I have had to struggle to keep from thinking of myself in the limiting way that word implies. So, for the record, I would like it known that I am not an "idiot." I am a person who suffers from idiocy. Nobody knows what it is like to deal with crippling bouts of idiocy while trying to lead a normal life. The last thing I need is for somebody to make it harder by pointing out what an "idiot" I am.

Here's an example of what I'm talking about: One day in December, I drove my wife to the bus stop. Before we got in the car, she gave me a greeting card for the cleaning people. I was to drop her off, go to the ATM, take out some cash, put it in the envelope with the card, and give it as a holiday thank-you to the cleaning people. I did not want the card rattling around in the front with me, so I opened the back door and laid the card in the middle of the back. The backseats had been folded down, and I put the card as far as possible from any crack it might slip into as a result of a swerve or a sudden stop.

While we were driving, my wife asked me for the card. She wanted to write a little note to the cleaning people and sign it. I told her the card was in the back. She turned around and saw it there. She undid her seat belt, crawled over her seat, and stretched out to reach it. She couldn't quite get to it, though, and she had to crawl even farther, until only her feet were in the passenger seat. She grabbed the card, and then eventually was able to slide back over the seat. Her clothes had become mussed, and I could tell that she was making an effort not to say what she thought.

Now, was it "idiotic" (her word, unspoken) of me to put

the card in the back, equidistant from hazardous cracks? Well, yes—and no. I believe I could argue both sides of this question, and convince you of the justice of either one. But I'm afraid that would only help to make my wife's larger point. Nobody but a moron, in other words, would even think about such idiotic topics. So I have decided that the wiser course is to drop the matter entirely.

By coincidence, just now I heard my wife downstairs reloading the dishwasher that I filled with breakfast and lunch dishes not half an hour ago. There were the sounds of dishes clattering and my wife shouting, "No! No! No!"

It's sad that my own wife has been taken in by the many misconceptions associated with people like me. Those of us unfortunate enough to be afflicted with idiocy are not grotesque caricatures or figures of fun. Idiocy can strike anybody, from the man who says he cleaned your chimney to the president of the United States. Very few of us conform to the old stereotype of the guy in the dunce cap sticking his finger in a light socket. (My wife notes, just parenthetically, that I did stick my finger in a light socket once.) Recently, I was reading a book by Dostoyevsky that I thought dealt with some of these issues in a sensitive way. It's called *The Idiocy Sufferer*, and I am happy to report that in this new translation the terms that cruelly objectify people like me have been updated more inclusively.

Of course, the story's hero, Prince Myshkin, lived in an earlier time and so had to wash his dishes by hand. At the moment, I don't remember whether he dried them with a dish towel or put them in a dish drainer to "air-dry." For people with our disorder, the drying phase seems to be the problematic one. Do you know what a garlic press is? (When telling this story, I've found it is always a good idea to ask.) A garlic press is a device that squeezes a clove of garlic through a grid of tiny holes. Many kitchens have one. This device is hand-operated and made of sturdy metal. You would think it could be put into a dishwasher like any similar utensil.

And that's true; it can. With this important caveat: you must first take out any adhering garlic fibers, those which remain pressed against the back part of the grid with the holes, or in the holes themselves. The dishwasher will not remove those fibers. They're too tightly packed against the thing, or something. And during the wash cycle the water will cause the garlic remnants to get all pasty against the metal, and then, when radiant heat bakes the dishes dry, the garlic fibers will be annealed and heat-sealed to the metal until there is virtually no way of getting them off.

My wife was standing over the sink when I came home from yoga the other day. She had the garlic press in one hand and a toothpick with a frayed end in the other. Broken tooth-picks littered the counter. She was picking, scraping, and generally scrabbling at the garlic press to remove the etc., etc. She has, in fact, mentioned this garlic-press problem to me before. She looked at me with an expression I have come to call her "death ray." I said something like "That's right, blame the victim," referring of course to my disorder. I see that we idiocy sufferers have much educating of the public left to do.